CAE Practice Tests 3

Student's Book

CAE

Practice Tests 3

*Past papers from the
University of Cambridge
Local Examinations Syndicate*

CAMBRIDGE
UNIVERSITY PRESS

Published by the Press Syndicate of the University of Cambridge
The Pitt Building, Trumpington Street, Cambridge CB2 1RP
40 West 20th Street, New York, NY 10011–4211, USA
10 Stamford Road, Oakleigh, Melbourne 3166, Australia

© Cambridge University Press 1995

First published 1995
Reprinted 1996

Printed in Great Britain
at the University Press, Cambridge

ISBN 0 521 55683 X Student's Book
ISBN 0 521 55682 1 Teacher's Book
ISBN 0 521 55681 3 Cassettes

Contents

Acknowledgements

The University of Cambridge Local Examinations Syndicate and the publishers are grateful to the following for permission to reproduce texts and illustrations. It has not always been possible to identify sources of all the material used and in such cases the publishers would welcome information from copyright owners.

The Independent on Sunday for the article on p. 2 (19.5.91); *The Independent* for the articles on p. 4 by Danny Danziger (5.11.90) on p. 27 (17.12.91) and on p. 75 (26.5.92); p.14 Octopus (part of Reed Books) for the extract from *Encyclopædia of Natural History* by Joyce Pope; p.19 and p.40 extracts reproduced by permission of Reader's Digest from *How is it done?* ©1990; p.18 extract from *Which?* July 1987, published by the Consumers' Association, 2 Marylebone Road, London NW1 4DF; *The Guardian* for the article on pp. 28-9 by Edward Greenfield (16.12.92) and on pp. 30-31 by Winston Fletcher (23.3.92); *New Internationalist* for the article on pp. 33-34 (October 1990); the extract on p.41 from *Awful Moments* by Philip Norman (Hamish Hamilton, 1986) copyright © Philip Norman 1986. Reproduced by permission of Hamish Hamilton Ltd; p. 51 Christopher Matthew for the article which was first printed in British Airways *High Life Magazine* (March 1992); p. 52-3 *Country Living* magazine/© National Magazine Company for the adapted extract from *Bringing up brock* (*Country Living*, April 1992); pp. 55-6 article published in *Which?* August 1989, published by the Consumers' Association (address as above). Freephone 0800 252100 for subscription details including how to obtain three free copies. This article was reprinted in *Essential Articles: The Journalism File* (Carel Press); p. 66 John Holt for the extract from his book *How Children Fail*, published by Penguin Books. Copyright © John Holt. p. 74 *The Observer* (29.9.92); p. 77 *BBC Wildlife Magazine* for the article from the July 1991 magazine; p. 79-80 © *The Telegraph* plc, London 1992; p.86 Gail Duff for the extract from her book *Herbs and Spices* published by Merehurst Books; p.89 Reed Consumer Books for the extract from *Let's Go Fishing* published by Treasure Press.

For permission to reproduce photographs: pp. C1 and C2: all pictures from Robert Harding Picture Library, photographers as follows: 1.5C and 1.5Q M. H. Black; 1.5D and 1.5R, 1.5F and 1.5L, 1.5G and 1.5N, 1.5H and 1.5M, 1.5I and 1.5O Roy Rainford; 1.5E and 1.5P Raj Kamal; 1.5J and 1.5K Philip Craven; p. C3 (top) Lincolnshire County Council: Usher Gallery, Lincoln, (bottom) Recreation, Leisure and Tourism Department, City of Lincoln; p. C4 (top left) Newcastle Evening Chronicle, (top right) Science Photo Library, (bottom left) Alex Bartel/Science Photo Library, (bottom right) Telegraph Colour Library; p. C5 (top left) Telegraph Colour Library, (top right) Liba Taylor/Panos Pictures, (bottom left)Trygne Bølstad/Panos Pictures, (centre right) Popperfoto, (bottom right) A. Warren/Telegraph Colour Library; p. C6 (bottom right) Telegraph Colour Library, all remaining pictures on this page: Robert Harding Picture Library, photographer (bottom left) Walter Rawlings, (top right) Gavin Hellier; pp. C7 and C10 Kenneth Griffiths; p. C8 (top left) Popperfoto, (top right) Robert Harding Picture Library, (centre left) Paul von Stroheim/Telegraph Colour Library; p. C9 (top left) Chris Stowers/Panos Pictures, (centre left) by permission of Barclay's Bank plc, (centre right) Jacqui and Peter Sanger/Telegraph Colour Library, (bottom right) Telegraph Colour Library; p. C11 Ged Murray; p. C12 Richard Waite; pp. C14 and 15 London Borough of Barnet; p. C16 (left) Popperfoto, (centre and right) Neil Hobbs.

Text artwork by Virginia Gray, Peter Ducker and UCLES.
Book design by Peter Ducker MSTD

To the student

This book is for candidates preparing for the University of Cambridge Local Examinations Syndicate (UCLES) Certificate in Advanced English (CAE) and provides practice in all the written and oral papers. It contains four complete tests based on CAE examinations set from 1992–1994. The examination consists of five papers as follows:

Paper 1   Reading   (1 hour and 15 minutes)

This paper consists of four texts selected to test a wide range of reading skills and strategies, with approximately 50 matching and multiple-choice questions.

Paper 2   Writing   (2 hours)

This paper consists of two writing tasks (e.g. letter, report, review, instructions, announcement, etc.) of approximately 250 words each. Section A consists of a compulsory task based on a substantial reading input.

   Section B consists of one task selected from a choice of four. Assessment is based on content, organisation and cohesion, accuracy and range of language, register and effect on target reader.

Paper 3   English in Use   (1 hour and 30 minutes)

This paper consists of six tasks designed to test the ability to apply knowledge of the language system, including grammar, vocabulary, register, cohesion, spelling and punctuation.

   Section A consists of multiple-choice and open-completion items based on two short texts designed to test control over formal elements of the language in context.

   Section B consists of questions requiring the revision or correction of two short texts, designed to test ability to refine and proof-read samples of written English.

   Section C consists of questions requiring the completion of a text and the expansion of notes into a fuller form, designed to test the ability to recognise, produce and organise written English which is appropriate to both purpose and audience.

Paper 4   Listening   (45 minutes)

This paper contains four texts of varying length and nature selected to test a wide range of listening skills with various types of matching, completion and multiple-choice questions.

Paper 5   **Speaking**   (15 minutes per pair of candidates)

The CAE Speaking Paper is conducted by two examiners (an Interlocutor and an Assessor), with pairs of candidates. The four phases of this paper are based on visual stimuli and verbal prompts and are designed to elicit a wide range of speaking skills and strategies from both candidates.

Fluency, accuracy and range of grammar and vocabulary, pronunciation, interaction and task achievement are assessed.

Practice Test 1

PAPER 1 READING (1 hour 15 minutes)

This paper requires you to read four texts and answer the accompanying questions.
For each question, choose one answer from the appropriate list of choices.

FIRST TEXT/QUESTIONS 1–9

Answer questions **1–9** *by referring to the newspaper article on page* **2** *about the sense of smell.*

For questions **1–9**, choose from list **A–D** the source in the article of each of the theories mentioned (**1–9**). Some choices may be required more than once.

1	Females are influenced by smell when choosing a mate.	**1** D (A)
2	Children learn to distinguish between good and bad smells by experience.	**2** B
3	Children like smells which adults regard as unpleasant.	**3** D
4	Young children judge the weight of objects primarily by size.	**4** A
5	Adults are better than children at judging smells.	**5** D
6	Children recognise smells from different sources.	**6** D
7	Smell can help children to recognise what something is made of.	**7** A
8	Babies can identify good and bad smells.	**8** A
9	The sexes differ in their ability to distinguish smells from an early age.	**9** A

A	Hilary Schmidt's experiments
B	the work of earlier researchers
C	future experiments by Hilary Schmidt
D	guessing unsupported by any known facts

Scents and sensibility

A sense of smell is something we are born with. Or is it?

Until recently, scientists believed that the commonsense view was wrong: research had suggested that we learn to distinguish between pleasant and unpleasant smells by experience. But child psychologists have taken a fresh look at these studies. The latest work on young children shows that it is not necessarily true that adults are 'better' at smelling than children.

Work on a child's sense of smell has more than academic value. Many accidental poisonings in the home happen because a child does not realise that certain smells, that of bleach for instance, should be associated with danger. Psychologists want to know whether telling children to avoid things that smell 'bad' is an effective way of warning them away from a potential poison. But crucial to this is whether children have the same ability as adults to distinguish between pleasant and unpleasant smells.

From early experiments that involved asking children between three and five years old what they thought of certain smells, researchers concluded that children must learn their appreciation of pleasant and unpleasant smells as they get older, rather than being born with it. One of the most surprising results of these tests was that the children said they liked the smell of synthetic sweat and faeces nearly as often as they said they liked banana.

Hilary Schmidt, a psychologist from the Monnell Chemical Senses Center in Philadelphia, understandably found this research hard to accept. She looked at the way the tests were conducted, and applied lessons from other work on child psychology to design her own experiments. She noted that children younger than five will often answer 'Yes' to leading questions even if the answers are contradictory. She therefore decided to set her experiment up as a game. She asked the children if they would give a particular smelly thing to Oscar the Grouch, a popular television character who lives in a dustbin and likes 'yucky' things, or to Big Bird, another television character who likes 'nice' things. She found that the children distinguished between pleasant and unpleasant smells in much the same way as an adult. With the help of younger and younger subjects, she hopes to discover the age at which babies and children are able to distinguish between smells; and perhaps shed light on the importance of the inherited component of the sense.

Could this work be of use in helping children to identify harmful substances around the house?

Children younger than seven or eight are notoriously bad at recognising what an object is from its shape alone. Schmidt points to an experiment she has carried out with children under five who were given a large styrofoam ball and a small, but heavy, lead ball to compare. After they had a chance to feel the two, she took the balls away, and showed them another pair of styrofoam and lead balls. When she asked them which of the two would be the heavier, they invariably pointed to the styrofoam ball just because it was bigger. Despite their earlier experience, they had not grasped the idea of what an object is made of – its substance – as well as size and shape. But in other experiments when she introduced odours, she found that children under five understood that smell was an important characteristic of substance, and children could use a scent to recognise substance irrespective of the shape or size in which it was presented to them.

Schmidt has also found that girls are more sensitive to smell than boys. The sex difference is well known in adults, but not in children. Explaining the difference in adults has centred on the suggestion that as girls get older, they tend to take part in activities such as cooking, which train them to distinguish between smells. Another suggestion was that after puberty, female hormones bring about some change in the olfactory equipment. But Schmidt's observation that the sex difference exists in children does not fit in with either explanation.

Because girls and boys apparently differ so much in their ability to smell, there may be a deeper evolutionary explanation. Schmidt hesitates to give her support to the idea, except to say: 'To speculate wildly beyond the available data, smell might be important for selecting a mate. In most species, the female chooses, while the male preens himself. Smell could be a primitive way of evaluating the human male.'

*For questions **10–15**, you must choose which of the paragraphs **A–G** below fit into the numbered gaps in the following magazine article. There is one extra paragraph, which does not fit in any of the gaps.*

WEATHERVANE MAKER

THE MAKING of weathervanes is an ancient skill, going back to early Egyptian times. Today the craft is still very much alive in the workshop that Graham Smith has set up. He is one of the few people in the country who make hand-cut weathervanes. Graham's designs are individually created and tailored to the specific requirements of his customers. 'That way I can produce a unique personalised item,' he explains. 'A lot of my customers are women buying presents for their husbands. They want a distinctive gift that represents the man's business or leisure interests.'

10 [ ]

It was not a cockerel but a witch on a broomstick that featured on the first weathervane Graham ever made. Friends admired his surprise present for his wife and began asking him to make vanes for them. 'I realised that when it came to subjects that could be made into them, the possibilities were limitless,' he says.

11 [B]

That was five years ago and he has no regrets about his new direction. 'My previous work didn't have an artistic element to it, whereas this is exciting and creative,' he says. 'I really enjoy the design side.'

12 [G]

Graham also keeps plenty of traditional designs in stock, since they prove as popular as the one-offs. 'It seems that people are attracted to hand-crafting,' Graham says. 'They welcome the opportunity to acquire something a little bit different.'

13 [ ]

'I have found my place in the market. People love the individuality and I get a lot of satisfaction from seeing a nondescript shape turn into something almost lifelike,' he says.

14 [ ]

'And nowadays, with more and more people moving to the country, individuals want to put an exclusive finishing touch to their properties. It has been a boost to crafts like mine.'

15 [ ]

American and Danish buyers in particular are showing interest. 'Pricing,' he explains, 'depends on the intricacy of the design.' His most recent request was for a curly-coated dog. Whatever the occasion, Graham can create a gift with a difference.

A Graham has become increasingly busy, supplying flat-packed weathervanes to clients worldwide.

B Graham decided to concentrate his efforts on a weathervane business. He had served an apprenticeship as a precision engineer and had worked in that trade for 15 years when he and his wife, Liz, agreed to swap roles – she went out to work as an architectural assistant and he stayed at home to look after the children and build up the business.

C It's all a far cry from the traditional cockerel, the most common design for weathervanes.

D Last month, a local school was opened with his galleon ship weathervane hoisted above it.

E 'For centuries, weathervanes have kept communities in touch with the elements signalling those shifts in wind direction that bring about changes in the weather,' he explains.

F Graham has no plans for expansion, as he wants to keep the business as a rural craft.

G Graham has now perfected over 100 original designs. He works to very fine detail, always seeking approval for the design of the silhouette from the customer before proceeding with the hand-cutting.

*Read the following newspaper article and answer questions **16–21** on page **5**.*
*Write the letter **A**, **B**, **C** or **D** against the number of each question. Give only one answer to each question.*

With the trees, I planted my stake in New Zealand

JONATHON PORRITT
TALKS TO
DANNY DANZIGER

Jonathon Porritt is the author of 'Seeing Green – The Politics of Ecology'.

I HAD a most peculiar period of my life when I didn't have any summers. I went out to New Zealand every summer here, which is the New Zealand winter, and so I had nine winters on the trot, which was great, because I like winter.

My parents came up with this idea of buying a small plot of land which 'the kids', my brother, sister and I, could look after. Mother said, 'If you can take the time and trouble to plant it with trees then you can have it.' The idea was that we would always have a stake in New Zealand, which is a lovely idea as my father was actually brought up there. And they found a plot of land about 20 miles north of Auckland in a place called Rangitoupuni. It's rather poor land, really, but it's quite good for planting trees on.

I've always been very keen and enthusiastic about land. I'd spent a year in Australia working on sheep stations and helping out in different farming jobs, and so the idea of planting trees sounded like a very nice idea, and I was immediately keen. I think the rest of the family got enthusiastic as we went along. I started planting in 1968, and by the end of 1972 between the three of us we'd planted the whole 70 acres.

In New Zealand in 1968 it was one of those winters. It rained an awful lot, endlessly in fact, and in a way it's idiotic to think back on it as such an immensely happy time as it rained pretty well most days that we were planting, and I don't suppose I've ever been wetter or colder for such a prolonged period.

There was a moment of truth every morning: getting ready for the next planting session. Coming out of the Land Rover relatively warm and dry, with the rain coming down, and your anorak still clammy from the day before, boots still sodden, hands fumbling with slippery laces.

> *'The brain begins to take over and to allow for all sorts of strange thoughts, ideas and reflections about life.'*

In that first year I had a guy to work with me who was an experienced tree-planter, which was very helpful as I'd never planted trees seriously before all this. You have a planting bag around your neck which you fill with as many trees as you possibly can, and when your bag is full it's a nightmare, and it's only as it gets lighter that life gets easier.

In a way, the most difficult bit of the entire operation was getting the lines straight. You work out what spacing you're going to plant the trees at, and then you line up a series of three poles across as long a trajectory as you can get, and those poles then determine your lines. Once you're in line, you just plant all the way down the line till you get to the end, turn around and come back again. I enjoy hard physical work, and it certainly made me fit.

After a certain point you can plant trees almost on automatic, you become used to a rhythm, and you use the minimum number of spade strokes that you need to get the hole in the ground. The rhythm is something that everybody tells you about and, of course, it's true of many agricultural jobs that you actually have to train the body into a series of quite standardised moves, and then it

becomes immensely easy: so you develop an absolutely regular process of taking the tree out of the bag, digging a hole, putting it in the ground, stamping it in, and moving on. Mentally, it's very interesting. The brain begins to take over and to allow for all sorts of strange thoughts and ideas and reflections about life – a lot of my thinking about the natural world and our place in it, all of those things that have since dominated my life, first began to pop through my head in those days.

I've been back to New Zealand four times since then and watched the trees gradually grow, which has been very satisfying when you actually planted the things and you do then have a kind of stake in what happens and how they prosper.

I always dread reading in the newspapers stories of another high wind in New Zealand, or *Worst Drought Ever Hits New Zealand*. Such headlines make me feel extremely apprehensive. However, it worked out extremely well and those trees are now 20 years old, and in good fettle.

The only postscript I should add is that I took a term off from teaching, and I went back there in 1984, completely on my own for three months. And I wrote my first book there, *Seeing Green*. There's a little cabin on the tree farm which is fantastically basic, just a bed, a table and a chair. In the mornings I would do my writing; in the afternoons I would go off and prune the trees, and then do research in the evenings.

The connection between me and that area is still immensely strong. In many respects it's the place that I feel most closely identified with in terms of that link between people and the earth: it's a most powerful bond.

16 When the Porritts first considered buying a piece of land for their children to look after,

    A Jonathon's brother and sister needed encouraging.
    B Jonathon himself reacted positively.
    C the whole family was equally enthusiastic.
    D Jonathon's mother imposed unrealistic conditions.

17 When he started planting trees in 1968, Jonathon

    A was employed by an expert tree-planter.
    B had experience of the work in Australia.
    C had only limited experience of tree-planting.
    D had to learn from scratch how to do the job.

18 1968 was a happy time for Jonathon even though

    A the work was physically demanding.
    B he didn't like being separated from his family.
    C the weather was very unpleasant.
    D he didn't enjoy living alone.

19 When did Jonathon become efficient at planting trees?

    A when he put fewer trees in his planting bag
    B when he got used to the nature of the soil
    C when he knew how to set up a planting line
    D when he had become accustomed to the routine

20 Jonathon found planting trees to be

    A the best way of keeping himself fit.
    B an increasingly monotonous activity.
    C a way to escape from reality.
    D an opportunity to reflect on important issues.

21 What is Jonathon's present view of the place where he lived in New Zealand?

    A He would like to spend more time there.
    B He would like to write about it.
    C He intends to return there soon.
    D He has a strong commitment to it.

16 ...

17 ...

18 ...

19 ...

20 ...

21 ...

FOURTH TEXT/QUESTIONS 22–42

Answer questions **22–42** *by referring to the holiday brochure on pages* **7–8**.

For questions **22–26**, choose from list **A–H** below the most suitable heading for each of the numbered sections (**22–26**) at the beginning of the brochure.

A	Different Modes of Travel	**E**	Be Independent
B	Easy for Everyone	**F**	Small Groups
C	What you Need	**G**	Who Travels with *Explore*?
D	Activities and Interests	**H**	Cultural/Adventure

For questions **27–34**, match the statement listed below with the appropriate holidays from list **A–G**. Some choices may be required more than once.
Note: When more than one answer is required, these may be given **in any order**.

You carry little with you.
27 .... **28** ....
You may stay with local people.
29 .... **30** ....
You need previous experience.
31 ....
You are taught what is required.
32 ....
You visit places that few visitors see.
33 .... **34** ....

A Wildlife and Natural History

B Ethnic Encounters

C Easy/Moderate Hiking

D Major Treks

E Wilderness Experience

F Sailtreks/Seatreks

G Raft and River Journeys

For questions **35–42**, match the statement listed below with the appropriate destinations from list **A–H**. Some choices may be required more than once.
Note: When more than one answer is required, these may be given **in any order**.

You may stay on a boat.
35 ....
You may leave the party for a short exploration.
36 .... **37** ....
You may be transported by experts.
38 ....
You may have your bags carried.
39 .... **40** .... **41** ....
You may travel by regular local transport.
42 ....

A Nepal

B Uganda

C the Dordogne River

D the Galapagos Islands

E the Alps

F Venezuela

G Zaire

H Thailand

Explore Worldwide
– small groups leave fewer footprints

Explore Worldwide is right in the forefront of adventure travel with trips designed for people who want to get more out of their holiday than just a beach. Our emphasis is on travel to new and unusual destinations, coupled with interesting and original itineraries. Our brochure contains over 100 original adventures – tours, treks, safaris and expeditions – in more than 60 countries around the world. Most trips last from 1–4 weeks.

22

Averaging 16 people. Small informal groups, expertly led. Giving you a real opportunity to discover more about the places we visit for yourself. More personal involvement brings you closer to the local scene and the local peoples. A stimulating experience for all travellers.

23

Many different kinds of transport are used. Often on the same trip. We travel by chartered coach or local bus, by train, expedition vehicle, minibus, boat, canoe, raft, camel, light plane etc. And often on foot. Each trip takes on the character of the local terrain.

24

Interesting people with the resilience to tackle new situations and get the most out of an original adventure. Mainly from the UK, Europe, Australia, New Zealand, Canada and the States. All our trips are designed to be within the capabilities of almost anyone who enjoys good health, is reasonably fit, and above all adaptable. The majority are aged between 25 and 55. About half are couples. The rest are enterprising individuals travelling alone.

25

It's not easy to describe *Explore Worldwide*. Each trip is completely unique. So we have divided our worldwide adventures into 8 different categories, describing some of the main activities and interests. Each category represents a special highlight that is an integral part of a particular tour, and of course trips have several different highlights. However, please bear in mind that many other factors contribute to the success of all our trips as a whole. Unique places, unusual encounters, strange customs, unpredictable events, personal involvement – all play their part in the full enjoyment of your holiday.

26

Almost all the trips in our brochure have a strong cultural feeling. But a certain number of tours have this as their primary emphasis, focusing closely on local cultures, ethnic peoples and classic sites. For example, anyone looking for destinations of outstanding cultural and historical interest should consider our trips in **Egypt, Jordan, Syria, Yemen, Turkey, Greece, India, Bhutan, Thailand, China, Peru, Bolivia, Guatemala and Belize** – to mention a few of the places featured in our programme! Short day walks of 2–4 hours to visit unusual or off-the-tourist-track sites are often an integral part of our trips.

Wildlife and Natural History

Our wildlife safaris visit many of the world's greatest game parks and offer a thrilling encounter with animals in their natural state. Choose from dozens of remarkable destinations. In **Africa**, for example, you often have the freedom to step outside your safari vehicle and tackle the wild terrain for yourself. You could track the rare silver-back mountain gorilla in **Zaire**, go bush walking with tribal guides in **Uganda**, climb **Mount Kenya**, ride a canoe on the **Zambezi River** or a traditional *mokoro* in the **Okavango Delta**. Most African safaris camp, and full camping equipment is provided. A few offer hotel and lodge accommodation throughout. Elsewhere, in **Asia and South America**, on trips which include game viewing – say, our tiger safari in **India** – we usually stay in hotels, resthouses and jungle lodges. In Darwin's famous **Galapagos Islands** we live aboard a small motor yacht.

Ethnic Encounters

A special highlight of an *Explore Worldwide* adventure is the opportunity it offers to meet ethnic or tribal peoples. These could be the 'Blue Men' or Tuareg of the **Central Sahara**, the Maya of **Mexico**, or the colourful Huli of **Papua New Guinea**. Some, like the Bushmen of the **Kalahari Desert**, are nomadic wanderers. Others, like the pygmies of the **Ituri Forest**, are hunter-gatherers; or dry rice farmers like the friendly hilltribe peoples of **Northern Thailand**. Many are often part of an 'Old World' culture. Their societies are often under serious threat from unscrupulous exploiters. We travel in small groups only. Our aim is to help spread tolerance and understanding between different races and peoples, with the minimum of cultural and environmental disturbance.

Easy/Moderate Hiking

Many trips include a few days' easy walking through open countryside, based on tented or hotel accommodation; also village-to-village hiking which involves some trail walking with the prospect of overnighting along the way in private houses or basic village huts. You'll find such trips in **Spain's Sierra Nevada**, in **Provence, Tuscany, Crete, Corsica, Greece, Morocco, Turkey, Bulgaria, Thailand, Bhutan, Nepal,**

Venezuela, and many other *Explore Worldwide* destinations. On long distance walks involving more than one day, all your main luggage is transported by a separate vehicle, or carried by porters or pack animals. You simply bring a daypack for your personal gear.

Major Treks

A limited number of major treks are offered for strong mountain walkers. These sometimes involve walking at elevations over 10,000 feet, with substantial altitude gains and losses during a single day. We may lodge with the local people or rough-camp in the world's great mountain ranges like the **Atlas, Kackar, Himalayas** and **Andes**. Or we use a mixture of well-appointed camp-sites and alpine chalets in more sophisticated mountain areas such as the **Alps**. Such trips usually involve support vehicles, porterage or pack animals. We rarely backpack or carry heavy gear.

Wilderness Experience

Discovering one of the world's remote wilderness areas is a thrilling and memorable experience – perhaps the ultimate travel adventure. Such places have a strong fascination for the intrepid traveller, holding out the prospect of exotic new horizons. We explore the haunting beauty of the **Amazon Rainforest** and experience the powerful mystique of the **Sahara, Great Thar, Namib** and

Gobi Deserts. They offer a chance to participate in an adventure few people could ever dream of.

Sailtreks/Seatreks

These are among the most original and relaxing holidays in our brochure. We charter local boats and journey by traditional *felucca* sailboat through **Upper Egypt**; we utilise *gulets* (wooden motor yachts) in **Turkey** and island-to-island ferries in countries like **Greece** and **Thailand**. Our 2-masted schooner explores the islands of the **Indonesian Archipelago**, while a small motor yacht is chartered to cruise among the unique wildlife habitats of the **Galapagos**.

Raft and River Journeys

River journeys can last from a few hours to several days, and range from 2-person inflatables which participants paddle themselves (on the **Dordogne River**, for example) to all the fun, thrills and excitement of whitewater rafting navigated by skilled oarsmen (such as on Peru's beautiful **Urubamba River** or the wild **Trisuli River** in **Nepal**). No previous experience is necessary and the appropriate safety skills are quickly learned. Our river trips in **India, Africa** and the **Amazon** offer us a unique insight into the fertile margins and exotic jungles.

Get your free copy of the Explore Worldwide brochure NOW!

PAPER 2 WRITING (2 hours)

*This paper contains one Section A task and four Section B tasks. You must
complete the Section A task and **one** task from Section B.
The two sections carry equal marks.
Read the task instructions and consider the information **carefully** both for
Section A and the task which you select for Section B.*

SECTION A

1   A fortnight ago you were on holiday in Scotland. One evening you went to
the cinema with a Scottish friend of yours, called Malcolm Taylor. On the
way home together, you witnessed an attempt by a young man to steal a
woman's handbag. Malcolm tried to help the woman and, although the thief
managed to run away, nothing was stolen. Malcolm suffered a bad cut to
his face. You have just received the letter below from Malcolm with the
newspaper cutting on page 10 enclosed.

*Read the letter and newspaper cutting and then, **using the information
carefully**, write the letter and note listed on page **10**.*

    … It was great to see you last month. I'm glad you enjoyed your holiday
– back at work now I suppose – hope it's not too boring! The reason I'm
writing is to ask you a favour. If you read the enclosed, you'll see it's
supposed to be a report about that incident outside the Rex Cinema, I'm
sure you'll remember it. Anyway, as you can see, they've given the
impression I was the mugger!! Whether it's just bad reporting or they've
missed a paragraph I can't make out, but the facts are all wrong – even
your nationality. Typical!

    I've phoned them and they say they'll print a correction, but I know that
just means a sentence hidden away at the bottom of one of the back
pages.

    Would you mind writing a letter to the paper, saying what really
happened?

    I think they'll print it if you've taken the trouble to write from abroad. I'd
be really grateful – all my family's friends read this local paper and the
report really makes me look bad.

    Many thanks. Keep in touch, hope to see you again soon.
Malcolm

> *EWENESS WEEKLY TIMES*
> *Wednesday May 27 1992*
>
> # Handbag Thief Caught
>
> A YOUNG MAN was arrested outside the Odeon Cinema in Grant Street last Thursday after attempting to snatch the handbag of a woman passer-by.
>
> Malcolm Taylor, 24, a Eweness resident, was accompanied by an American tourist who was not, however, involved in the incident. Miss Erskine, 27, suffered a cut to her face and was badly shaken. She said she was most upset by such an incident happening in a place like Eweness, but added 'I'm really most grateful to my rescuer.'

Write (a) *the letter to the 'Eweness Weekly Times' as requested by Malcolm (approximately* **200** *words)*

(b) *a relevant note to Malcolm (which you would attach to a copy of the letter) (approximately* **50** *words)*

You must lay these out in an appropriate way but it is not necessary to include addresses.

SECTION B

Choose **one** *of the following writing tasks. Your answer should follow exactly the instructions given. Write approximately* **250** *words.*

2   An English-speaking friend is going to stay in your home while you are on holiday. This is part of a letter which you receive from your friend.

> *'By the way, I hope I'll be able to watch TV while I'm staying at your flat. How does it work? How many channels will I be able to watch? What are the different channels like? Which programmes would you recommend me to watch? And are there any programmes which you think I should definitely avoid? Although I can't speak your language very well yet, I can understand quite a bit and think I should improve a lot by watching while I'm staying in your place ...'*

Write a **detailed note** which you leave in your home for your friend, covering **all the points** raised in the letter.

3 You have been asked to write an **article** for an international magazine about the status and care of the elderly.
Describe ways in which you think these have changed in your community over the past fifty years, and suggest developments you would like to see in the future.

4 This announcement has appeared in a local English language magazine.

Win a book token

Which three books would you most like to take with you if you were going to live on a desert island?

We are offering a prize for the best 250-word answer to this question.

The books you write about can be in any language but your answer must be in English. You should include **clear** descriptions of the books and an explanation of **why** they would be of special importance for you.

Write your **entry** for the competition.

5 Your boss has received the following request from a local school and has asked you to respond. Write a suitable **report** covering **all the points** mentioned by the students.

We are a class of High School students doing a project on recruitment and in-service training in different parts of the world. We should be very grateful if you or a member of your staff could spare the time to supply us with a brief report on how your company recruits new staff and trains them, and on what training opportunities it offers to existing staff.

PAPER 3 ENGLISH IN USE (1 hour 30 minutes)

This paper requires you to complete six tasks.
*Answer **all** questions.*
The total number of questions for tasks 1 to 5 is 63; the last task is numbered 81–88.

SECTION A

1   *For questions **1–15**, read the article below and then decide which word on page **13** best fits each space. Circle the letter you choose for each question. The exercise begins with an example (**0**).*

THE BEGINNINGS OF FLIGHT

The story of man's mastery of the air is almost as old as man himself, a puzzle in which the essential (**0**) ... were not found until a very late stage. However, to (**1**) ... this we must first go back to the time when primitive man (**2**) ... his food, and only birds and insects flew. We cannot know with any certainty when man first deliberately shaped weapons for throwing, but that (**3**) ... of conscious design marked the first step on a road that (**4**) ... from the spear and the arrow to the aeroplane and the giant rocket of the present (**5**) ... . It would seem, in fact, that this (**6**) ... to throw things is one of the most primitive and deep-seated of our instincts, (**7**) ... in childhood and persisting into old age. The more mature ambition to throw things swiftly and accurately, which is the origin of most (**8**) ... games, probably has its roots in the ages when the possession of a (**9**) ... weapon and the ability to throw it with force and accuracy (**10**) ... the difference between eating and starving.

It is significant that such weapons were (**11**) ... and brought to their (**12**) ... form at an early stage in history. If we were restricted to the same (**13**) ... , it is doubtful if we could produce better bows and arrows than those that (**14**) ... the armies of the past. The arrow was the first true weapon capable of maintaining direction over considerable (**15**) ... . It was to be centuries before man himself could fly.

---

0 (**A**) clues   **B** keys   **C** responses   **D** resolutions

1 **A** value   **B** approve   **C** understand   **D** realize

2 **A** pursued   **B** hunted for   **C** chased   **D** followed up

3 **A** act   **B** deed   **C** action   **D** event

4 **A** brings   **B** moves   **C** takes   **D** leads

5 **A** instant   **B** day   **C** hour   **D** moment

6 **A** feeling   **B** urge   **C** encouragement   **D** emotion

7 **A** coming   **B** arriving   **C** appearing   **D** growing

8 **A** exterior   **B** outside   **C** external   **D** outdoor

9 **A** suitable   **B** fitting   **C** related   **D** chosen

10 **A** involved   **B** meant   **C** told   **D** showed

11 **A** invented   **B** imagined   **C** planned   **D** produced

12 **A** last   **B** older   **C** latest   **D** final

13 **A** matters   **B** substances   **C** materials   **D** sources

14 **A** destroyed   **B** ruined   **C** spoiled   **D** exploded

15 **A** lengths   **B** extents   **C** areas   **D** distances

In the examination, your answer on the answer sheet would look like this:

0	A		**0**

2 *For questions* **16–30**, *complete the following article by writing each missing word in the space provided.* **Use only one word for each space.** *The exercise begins with an example* **(0)**.

EVOLUTION

It is generally accepted that present-day animals and plants differ from those of the past, **(0)** ....*having*...... changed by a general process called evolution. But this theory has been widely accepted for little **(16)** .... than a hundred years. The present theory of evolution was developed **(17)** .... two naturalists – Charles Darwin and Alfred Russell Wallace – working independently.

When he was a young man **(18)** .... 22, Darwin went as naturalist on a round-the-world, map-making cruise aboard a British naval survey ship, *HMS Beagle*. The cruise began in 1831 and lasted **(19)** .... 1836. In the Galapagos Islands, Darwin came **(20)** .... a group of birds, later to become known **(21)** .... 'Darwin's finches'. They were similar to one **(22)** .... in their colour, song, nests and eggs, and were clearly descended **(23)** .... the same finch stock, **(24)** .... each had a different kind of beak and was adapted **(25)** .... a different way of life. **(26)** .... were seed-eaters, fly-catchers, woodpeckers and various other types.

Darwin assumed that the ancestors of all **(27)** .... types had been blown to the islands in bleak weather, had survived and changed somehow **(28)** .... the various forms. In the years after the voyage, Darwin gradually came to the conclusion that individuals better suited **(29)** .... their environment would tend to leave more offspring while those **(30)** .... well adapted would die out.

In the examination, your answer on the answer sheet would look like this:

0	having	0
		▭ ▭

SECTION B

3 *In **most** lines of the following text, there is **one** unnecessary word. It is either grammatically incorrect or does not fit in with the sense of the text. For each numbered line **31–45** write the **unnecessary word** next to the question number. Some lines are correct. Indicate these lines with a tick (✓). The exercise begins with two examples (**0**).*

DISCOVERY OF STAINLESS STEEL

0	Stainless steel was discovered by (an) accident in 1913 by the British
0	metallurgist Harry Brearley. He was experimenting with steel alloys –
31	combinations of metals – that they would be suitable for making gun
32	barrels. A few months later he had noticed that most of his rejected
33	specimens had rusted although one was containing 14 per cent
34	chromium had not. The discovery led to the development of stainless steel.
35	Ordinary steel goes rusts because it reacts easily with oxygen in the air
36	to produce crumbly red iron oxides. Other metals, such as aluminium,
37	nickel and chromium, also react in a much the same way but
38	their oxides form an impermeable surface layer, stopping oxygen to
39	reacting with the metal underneath. With Brearley's steel, the
40	chromium formed such as a film, protecting the metal from further
41	attack. A variety of stainless steels are now made. One of the commonest
42	contains of 18 per cent chromium and 8 per cent nickel and is used
43	for kitchen sinks. Kitchen knives are made of steel containing about
44	13 per cent chromium. A very more corrosion-resistant alloy is
45	achieved by adding up a small amount of the metal molybdenum – these
	steels are used as cladding for buildings.

---

31 ...	**36** ...	**41** ...
32 ...	**37** ...	**42** ...
33 ...	**38** ...	**43** ...
34 ...	**39** ...	**44** ...
35 ...	**40** ...	**45** ...

In the examination, your answer on the answer sheet would look like this:

0	an	**0** ▭ ▭
0	✓	**0** ▭ ▭

4 *A medical student at university wants to obtain a temporary summer job in a hospital. For questions **46–57**, complete the **formal letter** to the Personnel Officer of the hospital, using the advice given in the **informal letter** from a friend who is a doctor at the same hospital. **Use one word only** for each gap. The words which you need **do not occur** in the informal letter. Write your answers in the spaces provided. The exercise begins with an example (**0**).*

LETTER FROM A FRIEND

Dear Anita,

Just a quick note to let you know that I've found out what you should do about getting a temporary job at the hospital.

Write to the Personnel Officer; his name is Mr I. Cooper. Tell him that you're looking for a temporary summer job and that you're wondering whether they need anyone. Mention that I suggested you write to him – I know him fairly well. Of course, he knows me as Dr Ferguson.

Tell him what you're doing now – you know, that you've been a medical student for about eighteen months – and that you'd really like to work in a hospital in your holiday because you've decided to become a hospital doctor when you get your degree.

Since you haven't done that sort of work before, you'd better tell him that you really want to learn and that you'll take anything they offer you.

I think you ought to put in your school certificates and your latest exam results from university because he'll probably want to see them. I wouldn't send the originals, though – you don't want them to get lost. And tell him that you'll send him any other info about yourself that he might want.

Finish the letter off by telling him where he can get in touch with you – you'll be at that address until mid-June, won't you?

Anyway, I must get back to work now.

Love,

James

LETTER TO PERSONNEL OFFICER

Mr I. Cooper   28, Highfield Place
Personnel Officer   Manchester
Archway Hospital
Manchester   14 January 1993

                                 Tel: 936574

Dear Sir,

   I am writing to **(0)** ....*enquire*.... whether you have any
(46) .... for temporary work. I have been
(47) .... to write to you by Dr James Ferguson.
   At present I am a **(48)** .... student at university,
taking a degree course in **(49)** ...., and I would very
much **(50)** .... the opportunity to work in a hospital
during my vacation, as it is my intention to become a
hospital doctor when I **(51)** ....
   Although I have not as yet had any **(52)** .... of this
type of work, I am very keen to learn and would be
willing to **(53)** .... any job you may be able to offer
me.
   I **(54)** .... photocopies of my school certificates
and of my most **(55)** .... examination results at
university. Should you require any further **(56)** ....,
I will be happy to send them to you. I can be **(57)** ....
until the middle of June at the above address and
telephone number. I look forward to receiving your
reply.

Yours sincerely

Anita Smithson

In the examination, your answer on the answer sheet would look like this:

0	enquire	0
		▭ ▭

SECTION C

5 *For questions* **58–63** *read through the following text and then choose from list* **A–J** *the best phrase or sentence given below it to fill each of the blanks. Write one letter* (**A–J**) *in the space provided.* **Some of the answers do not fit at all**. *The exercise begins with an example* (**0**).

WHEN HOTELS OVERBOOK

Ann Marshall booked a room at the Granada Hotel in London. She wrote to confirm and specifically asked the hotel to hold her room 'all night' as she would be arriving very late. So as to emphasize the fact, the hotel highlighted in their confirmation letter (**0**) ..J.. . So when Mrs Marshall arrived at the hotel at 11 pm on the night, she was astonished (**58**) ... . The staff arranged a room for her at another (inferior) hotel, and gave her £5 for taxi fares. Nevertheless, (**59**) ... . She got to bed later and had (**60**) ... . Above all, she didn't stay at the hotel of her choice. Hotels find themselves in something of a dilemma when demand for rooms is high, but they have rooms for guests (**61**) ... . Some hotels may be tempted to let booked rooms and hope that 'no-shows' will see them through. Airlines do the same when selling tickets on scheduled flights.

You are normally entitled to damages for breach of contract if a hotel at which you have a firm booking, especially one which they've confirmed in writing, refuses a room (**62**) ... . How much you're entitled to depends on the circumstances. The real point, though, is that if (**63**) ... , those who run hotels and airlines might be less inclined to overbook.

A she was expected to agree

B she was very put out

C to spend the night at a different hotel

D when you arrive

E who have not yet turned up

F you take the trouble to complain

G to be told it was full

H to get up earlier than she intended

I you do bother to book

J that a late arrival was expected

In the examination, your answer on the answer sheet would look like this:

0	J		0
			▭ ▭

6 You have been asked to write an article for a magazine. It is one of a series of articles entitled 'Famous English Poets'. Read the notes below and then use them to prepare the article. Write **no more than one sentence** for each numbered set of notes. Use connecting words and phrases as appropriate. You may add words and change the form of the words given in the notes but do not add any extra information. The first point has been expanded for you as an example (**0**).

LORD BYRON

0 *1788: born London, England. Father = 'Mad Jack' Byron, died when young B. 3 yrs old.*

81 *1796–98: Grammar School, Aberdeen.*
1801–05: Harrow School – member school cricket team.

82 *1805–09: Trinity College, Cambridge – early poetry published, mixed reactions.*

83 *1809–11: Sea journey to Greece via S. Portugal, S. Spain, Malta.*

84 *1812: Mediterranean experiences → poem 'Childe Harold's Pilgrimage' – overnight success, sudden fame.*

85 *1816: marriage to Anne Milbanke – separated after 1 year – then short stay in Switzerland.*

86 *1818: began masterpiece 'Don Juan' – 17 C. story – origins in folklore → long, narrative poem, 16 sections.*

87 *1823: 'Don Juan' completed – poem's individual flavour from*
(a) abrupt changes subject
(b) mixture themes – serious/comic.

88 *1824: travelled to Greece – deep involvement politics – sudden illness – died Missolonghi, Greece, 19 April.*

Example: 0 Lord Byron was born in 1788 in London, England, and his father was 'Mad Jack' Byron who died when the young Byron was three years old.

81

82

83

84

85

86

87

88

PAPER 4 LISTENING (approximately 45 minutes)

This paper requires you to listen to a selection of recorded material and answer the accompanying questions.
*There are four sections to the test, **A**, **B**, **C** and **D**. You will hear Section B **once** only. All the other parts of the test will be heard twice. During the test there will be a pause before each part to allow you to look through the questions, and other pauses to let you think about your answers.*

SECTION A

*You will hear a news report about storm damage in three regions, the South West, the South East and the North. The effects of this damage are listed. For questions **1–18**, put a tick (✓) in the box to indicate what has happened in each region. If nothing has happened, put a cross (✗).*
You will hear the recording twice.

		South West		South East		North
people trapped in cars	1		7		13	
people stranded at home	2		8		14	
animals in danger	3		9		15	
road or rail services affected	4		10		16	
electricity supplies affected	5		11		17	
reported fatalities	6		12		18	

SECTION B

*You will hear part of a telephone conversation in which a secretary is noting down details of an Open Day programme. As you listen you must fill in the information for questions **19–25**.*
*Listen very carefully as you will hear this piece only **once**.*

9.30	*Arrival*
	Welcomed by **19** _____
9.45	*Introductory film;* **20** _____
	in staff lounge.
	Followed by **21** _____
10.30	*Tour of* **22** _____
11.00	**23** _____ *: career structure*
	at AFG.
12.00	*Visit to* **24** _____
13.00	*Lunch with* **25** _____
14.00	*Depart*

SECTION C

*You will hear a radio interview with a young woman who runs her own restaurant. For questions **26–36**, complete the sentences with an appropriate word or short phrase.*
You will hear the piece twice.

Christine Patterson started running her own
restaurant | **26** | _____ |

In her first job she started work at | **27** | _____ |

She describes this as | **28** | _____ |

She often forgot whether or not she had remembered to add
the | **29** | _____ |

However, she learnt the importance of doing
things | **30** | _____ |

Christine's next job at 'The Gaiety' involved a lot
of | **31** | _____ |

She realised she was an important part of a | **32** | _____ |

She learnt to work faster by | **33** | _____ | against other staff.

In her own restaurant, the new things she had to learn were how to
manage | **34** | _____ | and
| **35** | _____ |

It's her opinion that women in catering are not sufficiently good
at | **36** | _____ |

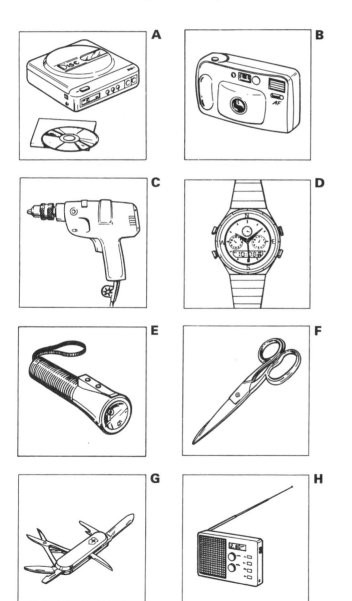

SECTION D

You will hear five short conversations in which people talk about various objects.

TASK ONE

For questions 37–41, look at the eight pictures labelled A–H. As you listen, put the pictures in order by completing the boxes 37–41 with the appropriate letter.

37	
38	
39	
40	
41	

TASK TWO

*Read the list of the purposes of each conversation. Decide which one on the list best describes each conversation you hear. For questions **42–46**, put the letter of the description against the appropriate conversation.*
You will hear the series twice.

What is the purpose of the conversation?

A   apologising for a mistake

B   complaining about something

C   describing something

D   explaining what he/she wants

E   expressing approval of something

F   checking something is suitable

G   making a promise

H   seeking help with a problem

Conversation 1	42	
Conversation 2	43	
Conversation 3	44	
Conversation 4	45	
Conversation 5	46	

PAPER 5 SPEAKING (15 minutes)

There will be two examiners, one acting as an Interlocutor and one as an Assessor. You will be examined, together with another candidate, referred to below as 'your partner'. One of you will be Candidate A and the other will be Candidate B.

Phase A (3 minutes)

You and your partner will talk about yourselves and each other. You will be asked to find out and offer information about you and your partner's background, interests, career plans, etc.

Phase B (3–4 minutes)

You will each be given the opportunity to talk for a minute. First you will be given the *same* set of two pictures (Past and present).
The Interlocutor will ask Candidate A to talk about the two pictures in a particular way and will explain this in full. The pictures are to be found in the centre section of this book on p. C3. Candidate A will have one minute to speak. Candidate B will listen carefully.
The Interlocutor will then ask Candidate B to respond to Candidate A's pictures in a particular way and will explain this in full.
Candidate B will have twenty seconds to speak.
You will then be given two new sets of pictures (Harbour scenes) on pp. C1 and C2 which are different from each other. The Interlocutor will give instructions to Candidates B and A. Candidate B will talk about the pictures in a particular way, for one minute. Candidate A will be allowed twenty seconds to respond to what has been said.

Phase C (3–4 minutes)

The Interlocutor will place a new set of pictures ('I could never...') on pp. C4 and C5 between you and your partner and will ask you to look at them together. These pictures provide the basis for a discussion between you and your partner. The Interlocutor will give instructions and you will have three or four minutes for this.

Phase D (3–4 minutes)

This will be based on what you have discussed in Phase C. You will first be invited to report the outcome of your discussion saying whether you agree or not with your partner. You will then take part in a more general discussion based on what has been discussed in Phase C. Both the Interlocutor and the Assessor will take part in this discussion.

Practice Test 2

PAPER 1   READING   (1 hour 15 minutes)

This paper requires you to read four texts and answer the accompanying questions.
For each question, choose one answer from the appropriate list of choices.

FIRST TEXT/QUESTIONS 1–15

*Answer questions **1–15** by referring to the magazine article about handwriting on page **27**.*

> *For questions **1–15**, match the handwriting characteristics (**A–J**) with the types of person listed (**1–15**). Some choices may be required more than once.*

1 a person who has recently had a shock	**A** writing that is not joined together
2 a person who dislikes company	**B** writing that ignores the accepted rules
3 a person who lacks confidence	**C** writing that has not been done firmly
4 a person who cannot be trusted	**D** writing that is well-formed
5 a person who is not lively	**E** unusually large letters
6 a secretive person	**F** a signature that has changed
7 a person who has committed a crime	**G** letters that are not formed separately
8 an honest person	**H** writing with a lot of capitals
9 a selfish person	**I** writing like that of a child
10 a confident person	**J** a very small signature
11 an emotional person	
12 a person with a medical problem	
13 a person of high intelligence	
14 a person with creative talent	
15 an emotionally immature person	

1 ...	**6** ...	**11** ...
2 ...	**7** ...	**12** ...
3 ...	**8** ...	**13** ...
4 ...	**9** ...	**14** ...
5 ...	**10** ...	**15** ...

The pen is mightier than the psychoanalyst
The study of handwriting to reveal a person's character is gaining support

If you applied for a job in some countries, you would almost certainly be asked for a sample of your handwriting. And it would be the handwriting, as much as anything else, that would determine your suitability for the job.

Handwriting analysis, or graphology, is accepted as a genuine science in many countries. Researchers say it can be a useful tool in indicating certain illnesses, such as heart disease and cancer, and can reveal psychological states and emotional disturbances.

Handwriting analysis is increasingly being used for vocational guidance and as an adjunct to interviews. Many big companies now employ graphologists to analyse the handwriting of potential candidates for key jobs.

But most doctors and psychiatrists remain dubious about the value of graphology. Patricia Marne, a professional graphologist for more than 20 years, argues that they should take it more seriously. She believes that handwriting can indicate psychological characteristics as well as certain medical conditions.

She says: 'Handwriting is a powerful indicator of social class and intelligence. But more than that, it can be used to assess mental ability and potential, whether a person should concentrate on arts or sciences, and whether they have a devious or open character.'

According to Ms Marne, graphology can be particularly useful in assessing possible criminal tendencies: 'Criminals all have disturbed handwriting, mostly illiterate and poorly-shaped. Most criminals come from deprived backgrounds and have arrested emotional development. This often shows up in unusually childish handwriting and in going over letters several times.

'Young male offenders frequently have very high ascenders, indicating that they live in a world of fantasy and dream of making it big. Graphologists can tell whether violence is about to erupt, whether the writer is under unbearable pressure, and whether there are psychopathic tendencies. Handwriting can be used to predict would-be suicides.'

Heart and lung problems can also show up, she says. 'You can't make a diagnosis from one sample, unless the writing is obviously shaky or disturbed. But if over a period of time it changes or becomes disjointed, if there's a break in the signature which did not exist previously, that could be a sign that something quite serious has occurred.'

A severe emotional upset can also show up in a temporarily altered signature, she maintains.

Ms Marne says handwriting can be used to reveal other psychological characteristics. People with writing in which letters form 'threads' instead of being individually formed are, apparently, devious and clever. Those who write mainly in capitals are trying to conceal their true selves from others. Very light pressure indicates sensitivity and lack of vitality. Originality in handwriting – how far the writer has deviated from copybook script – indicates confidence and artistic ability. Disconnected writing is the cardinal sign of the loner.

Very small signatures indicate inhibition and an inferiority complex; circles over the 'i' are a bid for attention, and crossing the 't' heavily over the whole word is a sign of intolerance and a patronising attitude.

Ms Marne says it takes six years of study and experience to be able to analyse handwriting accurately, and this has to be combined with empathy and intuition. She feels that more research is needed to put graphology on a proper scientific footing.

This will happen soon, she believes. 'It's actually far more accurate than psychoanalysis, as you can tell the whole history of the person, including all their emotional crises, without asking them questions to which they may give wrong answers.'

Interesting as all this may sound, there is little hard evidence to support such claims. Some psychiatrists are highly critical of them. Handwriting, they say, is a product of education, artistic ability and the type of writing taught – and has no other significance.

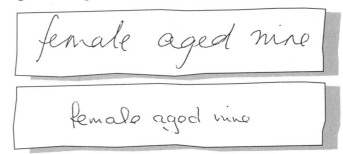

The person behind the handwriting: examples analysed by graphologist Patricia Marne. "I can tell whether people are honest, manipulators, or reliable employees."

SECOND TEXT/QUESTIONS 16–21

*For questions **16–21**, you must choose which of the paragraphs **A–G** on page **29** fit into the numbered gaps in the following magazine article. There is one extra paragraph, which does not fit in any of the gaps.*

A trumpet isn't just for Christmas ...

It is strange how many musicians, even leading ones, come from homes without music. Out of the blue, Hakan Hardenberger, the only son of totally unmusical parents in a country district of Southern Sweden, has at the age of 30 established himself as unique among the world's trumpet-players today.

16

Recently in one of London's premier concert halls he played the Hummel Trumpet Concerto, something of a party-piece for him, while on television a whole feature was devoted to his work and development, filmed both here and in Sweden.

Born near Malmo, he owes his career to the accident of a Christmas present when he was only eight.

17

The success of the gift was instant. The boy never stopped playing. His mother managed to contact the second trumpet-player in the Malmo Symphony Orchestra, whom she persuaded to give her son lessons.

18

There the mature Hardenberger has to draw a line between himself and his teacher. 'The trumpet is so primitive an instrument,' he explains, 'that you can't build a trumpet that is acoustically perfect. Whatever you do, it will have imperfections. Besides, you can't find two mouthpieces exactly the same. To me it is a matter of getting to know the imperfections and making a relationship with them.'

19

And unlike the great British contender among virtuoso trumpet-players, John Wallace, who developed originally from a brass-band background and then through working in orchestras, Hardenberger has always thought of himself as a solo artist pure and simple.

20

His parents gave him every chance to practise, and went along with his ambition to make trumpet-playing a career. It was then a question of where, at 15, he should be sent to study. America, Bo Nilsson's first choice, was thought to be too far away and too dangerous, which meant that he went instead at the age of 16 to study in Paris with Pierre Thibaud. Thibaud confirmed his prejudice against going into an orchestra, saying that 'Playing in the orchestra is like digging in the garden.'

21

Thibaud suggested that he should enter the competition 'just for experience'. Hardenberger learned the pieces for the first round only, but he won through to the second. Luckily he already knew most of the pieces in that round too, but on getting through to the final he was faced with a concerto that had already daunted him. He didn't win first prize that time, but he enjoyed the performance, realising that though he 'played like a pig', people did listen to him.

Quoted like that, Hardenberger's realism about his work and his career may sound arrogant, but that would be a totally false impression. Thoughtfully he refuses to try and analyse what such a gift of communication might consist of, as 'You risk destroying it in trying to explain. The power of the music lies in the fact that it can always move people.'

A From the very start Hardenberger seems to have had the gift of finding the right compromise, and making that relationship. Without any sense of boasting, he explains that even in his boyhood years the characteristic Hardenberger sound was already recognisable, 'the first thing I acquired'.

B He is always anxious to extend his repertoire. Hans-Werner Henze is the latest composer to be writing a piece for him, while on other records he has unearthed rare works from the 17th and 18th centuries.

C He was objective enough about himself to know that he played the trumpet better than others of his age, but it was only at the end of the first competition he entered, at the age of 17 during his first year in Paris, that he came to realise that in addition he had a particular gift of communicating.

D His father, unmusical but liking Louis Armstrong's playing, had the idea of giving his only son a trumpet. Being a serious man, he didn't pick a toy trumpet, but took advice and bought a genuine grown-up instrument.

E His records are continually opening up new repertory, not just concertos by long-neglected composers of the baroque and classical periods, but new works too. When you meet him, bright-eyed and good-looking, he seems even younger than his years, as fresh and open in his manner as the sound of the trumpet.

F Bo Nilsson was an up-and-coming musician, and at once spotted natural talent. Hardenberger consistently blesses his luck to have got such a teacher right from the start, one who was himself so obsessed with the trumpet and trumpet-playing that he would search out and contact players all over the world, and as a 'trumpet fanatic' was 'always looking for another mouthpiece'.

G From early boyhood he had as a role-model the French trumpeter, Maurice André, another player who bypassed the orchestra. The boy bought all his records, and idolised him.

THIRD TEXT/QUESTIONS 22–26

Read the following newspaper article and answer questions 22–26 on page 31.
Indicate the letter A, B, C or D against the number of each question, 22–26. Give
only one answer to each question.

Hit and miss of mass marketing

AS ALMOST everyone knows, advertising is in the doldrums. It isn't just the recession. Advertising started to plummet early in 1989, well before the recession really began to bite.

Advertising's problems are more fundamental, and the decline is worldwide. The unhappy truth is that advertising has failed to keep up with the pace of economic change.

Advertisers like to think in terms of mass markets and mass media; but as brands and media have proliferated, target markets have fragmented. Even campaigns for major brands ought to be targeted at minority audiences, but they rarely are. That is the principal way in which advertising has gone astray.

Think about your own shopping habits. If you visit a supermarket you may leave with 30, 40 or perhaps 50 items listed on your checkout bill, the average number of items of all kinds purchased per visit of all kinds.

Many of these will not be advertised brands; some others will be multiple purchases of the same brand. At a maximum you will have bought a handful of advertised brands from the 15,000 lines on sale in the store. Over a year you are unlikely to buy more than a few hundred brands.

Consumer durables? Perhaps a dozen a year. Cars? If yours is a new car, the statistical likelihood is that it is supplied by your employer.

If it isn't, you only buy one every three years. And though it may seem otherwise, you do not buy that many clothes either, and most of them will not be advertised brands.

Even when you throw in confectionery, medicines, hardware, all the services you can think of, it is virtually certain you do not buy more than 400 different brands a year. Compare that figure with the 32,500 branded goods and services that, according to Media Register, are advertised. Let's ignore the 23,000 which spend less than £50,000 a year, and concentrate on the 9,500 brands that Media Register individually lists and analyses.

Mr and Mrs Average have bought 400 of that 9,500, and not all because of their advertising. That's about 4 per cent. So you can forget that naive claim usually attributed to Lord Leverhulme: 'Half of my advertising is wasted but I've no way of knowing which half.' You could say that 96 per cent of all advertising is wasted, but nobody knows which 96 per cent.

When you're watching TV tonight, count how many of the commercials are for brands you buy or are likely to buy in the future. For most people the figure seems to be about one in 16 (6 per cent) so the commercials for the other 15 (94 per cent) are, on the face of it, wasted.

You probably think you're a spe-

cial case, that you are impervious to advertising. Almost everyone thinks the same. But you aren't and they aren't. The truth is nobody buys most of the brands they see advertised.

Waste is inherent in the use of media for advertising. The notion that every reader of a publication or every viewer of a commercial break might immediately rush out and buy all or even many of the brands advertised is ludicrous. People register only a tiny number of advertisements they see and ignore the rest, so waste cannot be avoided. That does not mean advertising isn't cost-effective. Millions of advertisements have proved it is.

Advertising has to communicate with large numbers of people to reach the relevant minority, because the advertiser cannot know, in advance, exactly which individuals will respond to his blandishments. Media advertising works, despite its much publicised expense, because it is a cheap means of mass communication.

Nonetheless, all waste is gruesome. With smart targeting the advertiser can minimise the wastage by increasing the *percentage* of readers or viewers who will respond; but he can never know *precisely* who will respond. Even the most accurate and finely tuned direct mail-shot never achieves a 100 per cent response. This is one of the fundamental differences between the use of media and face-to-face selling. It is possible, just, to envisage a salesman scoring with every prospective client he speaks to. The same could never happen when media are used. If the advertiser knew exactly which people were going to respond there would be no point in using media at all. The advertiser could communicate with them directly.

This is as true of Birth, Marriage and Death notices as it is of soft drink commercials. Any advertiser who can net one million new customers (2 per cent of the adult population) is doing well. Of soap powder, the two top-selling brands in supermarkets would be delighted with a million extra customers. So that any advertising campaign, for any product (or any political party for that matter) which could win over 2 per cent of the population would be outstandingly successful: and that, as I began by saying, is but a tiny minority of the population.

The most cost-effective way to reach them may be the use of mass media, but if advertising is to get going again its message will need to be more tightly targeted than ever before.

22 How can advertisers cut down on waste?
  A by using more face-to-face, direct selling techniques
  B by advertising through the mail rather than on TV
  C by aiming their advertising at particular groups of consumers
  D by using mass media advertising for certain types of products only

23 Advertising seems to be effective for
  A about half of all products.
  B many well-known brands.
  C very few products.
  D the most heavily advertised products.

24 Advertising through TV and other media is considered worthwhile because
  A a huge number of people see the adverts.
  B consumers are influenced far more than they realise.
  C it is easy to target a specialised audience.
  D people respond immediately to TV advertising.

25 One of the advertising industry's problems is that
  A manufacturers are not spending enough on their campaigns.
  B there are too many good quality products on the market.
  C nowadays consumers have less money to spend.
  D marketing is not sufficiently well-directed.

26 In order to be successful, advertisers need to
  A research carefully who is most likely to buy the product.
  B achieve only a small percentage increase in sales.
  C consider which type of advertising will be most effective.
  D target the widest possible audience among the adult population.

22 ...

23 ...

24 ...

25 ...

26 ...

FOURTH TEXT/QUESTIONS 27–42

Answer questions 27–42 by referring to the article about apples on pages 33–34.

For questions 27–35, answer by choosing one of the apples in list A–G. Some choices may be required more than once.

Which apple

27   got its name because it looked like another fruit?

28   was a very small size?

29   was a Roman apple suited to the English climate?

30   gave its name to a trade?

31   contributed to the development of a new cultivation system?

32   was used as a cooking apple for centuries?

33   was found growing among things that had been thrown away?

34   had its name changed as a result of an appreciative comment?

35   was different in colour from earlier apples?

A   wilding

B   Decio

C   Pearmain

D   Costard

E   Pippin

F   Delicious

G   Granny Smith

For questions 36–42, answer by choosing from the list of people A–G. Some choices may be required more than once.

Who

36   returned from a successful mission abroad?

37   was the subject of many stories?

38   noticed something strange about a dead tree?

39   sent a representative to learn about growing techniques abroad?

40   became the provider for the family?

41   valued apple-pips very highly?

42   explained the development of a particular apple in religious terms?

A   Romans

B   Henry VIII

C   Richard Harris

D   settlers

E   John Chapman

F   Jesse Hiatt

G   Maria Anne Smith

27 ...   30 ...   33 ...
28 ...   31 ...   34 ...
29 ...   32 ...   35 ...

36 ...   40 ...
37 ...   41 ...
38 ...   42 ...

A history of the apple

Apples have been with us since the dawn of recorded time, in countless varieties of colour, shape and size. But the late twentieth century is in danger of squandering its heritage.

1 Prehistoric wildings 8,000 BC

Human beings have been munching apples since prehistoric times. They spat out apple-pips in neolithic Britain. And 10,000 years ago they left apple remains to carbonise around their Swiss and Italian lakeside homes. In Switzerland and in the regions adjoining the Caucasus mountains, ancient humans even appear to have dry-stored apple-halves for winter. But these were wild crab apples, tiny wizened fruit which, in Ancient Britain, came to be known as 'wildings'. They had little in common with the apples we know today.

2 Norman knowledge 1000 AD

From the Romans the French learned great fruit-growing skills which were developed in the monasteries. This knowledge, which included expert cider-making, was taken to Britain from Roman times, like the dessert apple, Decio – thought to have been introduced by the Roman general, Etio. But most Roman varieties were unsuitable for the British climate and the Norman varieties rapidly took precedence. British monks continued experimenting and developing new apples, and it is from these varieties that Western apples are largely descended.

3 Mediaeval favourites 1200

Several kinds of apples became established in Britain during the thirteenth century. The Old English Pearmain, recorded in 1204 and so named because of its pear-like shape, was the main dessert apple until well into the eighteenth century. Its cooking partner was the Costard, which was sold in the markets of Oxford from 1296 until the end of the seventeenth century and gave us the word 'costermonger' – meaning someone who sells fruit and vegetables in the street. But prosperity declined as the country was hit by successive droughts, the Black Death and the Wars of the Roses. Fewer apples were produced and more were imported. This went on until the sixteenth century when Henry VIII ordered his chief fruiterer, Richard Harris, to visit France and learn about apple cultivation. Harris returned with a 'great store of grafts' including the famous Pippins, from which he grew the first ever modern-style orchard at Teynham in Kent.

4 Settler treasure 1750

By the seventeenth century apples were so popular in Britain that the first settlers who sailed to Canada, Australia, the US, South Africa and New Zealand took apples and apple-pips with them, counting these among their most treasured possessions. Captain Bligh of the Bounty took the first apples to Australia; Jan van Riebeeck, the founder of Cape Settlement, took them to South Africa and the Pilgrim Fathers who boarded the Mayflower carried them to America. In North America the most famous apple-planter was John Chapman, or 'Johnny Appleseed'. Born in 1774, he planted seedling nurseries from Pennsylvania in the east through

Ohio into Indiana in the west. The Indians regarded him as a medicine man and his apple-tree enthusiasm, odd clothing and religious devotion – he distributed religious tracts torn in parts for widespread circulation – started many folktales. He was said, for example, to be so kind to God's creatures that he even slept with bears.

5 Modern Delicious 1850

About this time in Iowa, a Quaker farmer called Jesse Hiatt discovered something sprouting from the roots of a dead tree. The shoot grew into an apple tree bearing a totally new apple which Hiatt named 'Hawkey'. He sent it to a fruit show and on biting into one the judge exclaimed 'Delicious, delicious!'. In 1895 the apple was introduced to the trade as a 'Delicious' and became one of the most widely grown apples in the world.

6 Granny Smith 1850

Another of the most famous modern apples was discovered in Australia by Maria Anne Smith. The daughter of transported convicts, Maria was fiercely independent, rejecting both the criminal life of her parents and the bureaucratic hypocrisy of the colonial administration. She worked as a midwife in the small township of Eastwood in New South Wales, where she was known as 'Granny-Smith' because she took on responsibility for maintaining the farm and orchard, which was the family's main source of income. One day in 1868 she found a small tree pushing its way through a pile of discarded fruit. She transplanted it and before long was harvesting the world's first major crop of green apples, soon to be famous all over the world. When asked how the tree came about she said, 'Well, it's just like God to make something useful out of what we think is rubbish' – a comment which referred not only to the fruit but also her own convict origins.

7 Uniformity rules 1950

Apples are now grown all over the world from Himachal Pradesh in northern India to small luxury orchards throughout Africa. Most, though, are grown commercially and come from just half a dozen varieties – usually chosen for their red skin or because they travel well rather than because they taste good. A plague of uniformity is sweeping the world, numbing the taste-buds and reducing the gene pool. While amateur gardeners in the UK have kept many old apple varieties alive, the US has lost forever most of the apples it had 100 years ago.

But consumers are starting to demand more variety. We can't leave the responsibility of saving diversity in our apples – or any other food – up to the random selections of amateur gardeners. We must insist on a world where natural diversity is valued and protected for the benefit of all.

PAPER 2 WRITING (2 hours)

*This paper contains one Section A task and four Section B tasks. You must
complete the Section A task and **one** from Section B.
The two sections carry equal marks.
Read the task instructions and consider the information **carefully** both for
Section A and the task which you select for Section B.*

SECTION A

1   You are studying English at a local institute of education. As part of your
     course you have to do a special project on some aspect of the English
     language. One day you receive three notes related to your project.
     Read the notes carefully and then, **using the information given**, write the
     three letters listed on page **36**.

> *Can I just remind all my students who have chosen
> the special project on 'Varieties of English Around
> the World' that they should be giving that piece of
> work to me by the end of this month? I would like
> to keep strictly to this deadline, so remember, you
> have only about 4 weeks left!*
>   *J.R.K.*

THE ENGLISH LIBRARY

We regret to inform you that we have been unable to
locate a copy of:

The English Spoken in India
Author: V. J. SINGH

It is possible for us to make further enquiries
through the inter-library loans system, but as this
may well take 6 to 9 weeks, we would ask you to
confirm that you would like us to proceed.

How's your project on the English spoken in India going? Sounds interesting, even if you are finding the research a little hard to do. Maybe I can help. It occurs to me that books may not be all you need! I have a terribly intellectual aunt who's a great traveller, and takes a keen interest in all kinds of aspects of the places she's been to. She was actually born in India, and I think, if you ask her nicely, she'll be able to give you all kinds of examples of how English is used there. She could certainly tell you about words and idioms which are only used in India, and about things like pronunciation and any differences in grammar. In fact, I can mention it to her myself, but I think you should write her a letter, telling her what you're doing, and asking her if she can give you some details and examples. Don't forget to tell her you're an old friend of mine! She's called Kumari Patel (perhaps you'd better call her Dr Patel!) and her address is 32 John St, Newhall, Cheshire.

All the best

Meena

Now write

    *(a) a postcard to the English library (write about **50** words)*

    *(b) a note to Meena (write about **50** words)*

    *(c) a letter to Dr Patel (write about **150** words)*

SECTION B

*Choose **one** of the following writing tasks. Your answer should follow exactly
the instructions given.*
*Write approximately **250** words.*

2   This is part of a letter that you receive from a friend.

> *'As you know, I finish school this summer and I'm looking forward
> to starting work and earning some money of my own. Eventually I
> want to open my own shop and intend to get a job in the local
> department store straightaway to gain as much practical
> experience as possible. Of course my parents want me to go to
> college and do a business course but I feel I'd learn more on the
> job. My brother suggests I spend a year travelling before I make up
> my mind – so I could even go to Australia or somewhere and
> improve my English. Please let me know what you think ...'*

Write to your friend, **giving practical advice**, referring to the points in the
letter.

3   You have been asked by a college magazine to write **an article** entitled 'How
to enjoy yourself without spending a fortune'.
Write the article. You should describe a range of free or inexpensive
activities available in your town, recommending those activities which you
personally feel are best suited to new students.

4   You have just seen the following advertisement.

> ## ARE YOU HIGHLY RESPONSIBLE & RESOURCEFUL?
>
> Individual or couple required to live in our beautiful house in English
> countryside, large gardens, swimming pool etc. for three months.
> We shall be abroad on business and you will have to supervise painters
> and decorators, keep the gardens tidy and deal with phone calls.
> To live in luxury, rent-free, write giving details of why we should entrust our
> house to you, with the names of two referees, to
> P.O. Box 423, Rainton, Hants.

Write your **application** for this position giving relevant information about
yourself.

5   An English friend is going to stay in your flat while you are away. You have
always helped your elderly next-door neighbour, who can be rather difficult.
You would like your friend to continue helping him/her during your
absence. Write some **notes** to leave for your friend, giving particular
information and advice on how to deal with the neighbour.

PAPER 3 ENGLISH IN USE (1 hour 30 minutes)

This paper requires you to complete six tasks.
*Answer **all** questions.*
The total number of questions for tasks 1 to 5 is 63; the last task is numbered 81–89.

SECTION A

1 *For questions **1–15**, read the article below and then decide which word on page **39** best fits each space. Circle the letter you choose for each question. The exercise begins with an example (**0**).*

THE LANGUAGE OF TEARS

The ability to weep is a uniquely human form of emotional response. Some scientists have suggested that human tears are (**0**) ... of an aquatic past – but this does not seem very likely. We cry from the moment we enter this (**1**) ... , for a number of reasons. Helpless babies cry to (**2**) ... their parents that they are ill, hungry or uncomfortable. As they (**3**) ... they will also cry just to attract parental attention and will often stop when they get it.

The idea that (**4**) ... a good cry can do you (**5**) ... is a very old one and now it has scientific (**6**) ... since recent research into tears has shown that they (**7**) ... a natural painkiller called enkaphalin. By (**8**) ... sorrow and pain this chemical helps you to feel better. Weeping can increase the quantities of enkaphalin you (**9**) ... .

Unfortunately, in our society we impose restrictions upon this naturally (**10**) ... activity. Because some people still regard it as a (**11**) ... of weakness in men, boys in particular are admonished when they cry. This kind of repression can only increase stress, both emotionally and physically.

Tears of emotion also help the body (**12**) ... itself of toxic chemical (**13**) ... , for there is more protein in them than in tears resulting from cold winds or other irritants. Crying comforts, calms and can be very enjoyable – (**14**) ... the popularity of the highly emotional films which are commonly (**15**) ... 'weepies'. It seems that people enjoy crying together almost as much as laughing together.

0	**A**	witness	**(B)**	evidence	**C**	result	**D**	display

1	**A**	world	**B**	place	**C**	earth	**D**	space
2	**A**	communicate	**B**	persuade	**C**	inform	**D**	demonstrate
3	**A**	evolve	**B**	change	**C**	develop	**D**	alter
4	**A**	doing	**B**	making	**C**	getting	**D**	having
5	**A**	better	**B**	fine	**C**	good	**D**	well
6	**A**	validity	**B**	truth	**C**	reality	**D**	reason
7	**A**	contain	**B**	retain	**C**	hold	**D**	keep
8	**A**	struggling	**B**	fighting	**C**	opposing	**D**	striking
9	**A**	construct	**B**	achieve	**C**	provide	**D**	produce
10	**A**	curing	**B**	treating	**C**	healing	**D**	improving
11	**A**	hint	**B**	symbol	**C**	feature	**D**	sign
12	**A**	release	**B**	rid	**C**	loosen	**D**	expel
13	**A**	rubbish	**B**	waste	**C**	leftovers	**D**	remains
14	**A**	consider	**B**	remark	**C**	distinguish	**D**	regard
15	**A**	named	**B**	entitled	**C**	subtitled	**D**	called

In the examination, your answer on the answer sheet would look like this:

0	B		0
			▭ ▭

2 *For questions* **16–30**, *complete the following article by writing each missing word in the space provided.* **Use only one word for each space**. *The exercise begins with an example* (**0**).

ROBOTS

The popular idea of a robot is a machine that acts (**0**) ..like...... and resembles a human being. But the robots that are increasingly (**16**) .... used for a wide range of tasks do not look human-like (**17**) .... all. The robots (**18**) .... work in car factory production lines look something like cranes. The mobile robots used (**19**) .... army bomb-disposal squads look like wheel barrows on tracks. And children (**20**) .... likened a mobile robot used in school to teach (**21**) .... computer programming to a giant sweet. Robots (**22**) ...., however, resemble human beings in the range of actions that they can carry out. Instead of repeatedly performing (**23**) .... one action, like an automatic machine, a robot can perform (**24**) .... chain of different actions. Its movements are controlled (**25**) .... by oil or air pressure or by electric motors, and its brain is a small computer that directs its movements. Inside the computer's memory (**26**) .... the instructions (**27**) .... carrying out a task – picking chocolates from a container and putting them in the right part of a display box, for example. By changing the programme, the robot can (**28**) .... made to vary the task, or do (**29**) .... different within the limits of the activities it is designed (**30**) ....

In the examination, your answer on the answer sheet would look like this:

0	like	0
		▭ ▭

SECTION B

3 *In **most** lines of the following text, there is **one** unnecessary word. It is either grammatically incorrect or does not fit in with the sense of the text. For each numbered line **31–45**, write the **unnecessary word** in the spaces next to the question number below. Some lines are correct. Indicate these lines with a tick (✓). The exercise begins with two examples (**0**).*

WANTED

0	'Wanted' ran a small ad in *The Times*. 'Assistant for the famous cookery
0	writer. Three-month contract – £400'. The ad was answered by a young
31	woman, recently widowed and with a small baby, desperate to for work
32	of any kind. The hours were long and £400 seemed very little for three
33	months' of employment. But she was desperate and she got
34	the job. It proved harder than she had been anticipated, as the famous
35	writer proved as tyrannical, ungrateful and a slave-driver. The first
36	week of helping to him was almost more than the young woman could
37	stand. Only did the thought of the bread that she was putting in her
38	baby's mouth prevented her leaving from the job. At the end of the
39	first terrible week, she was given a lift to home by the cookery writer's
40	secretary. On the way home she confided how desperately she had
41	needed the job and admitted how welcome would it be even the
42	miserable £400 was mentioned in the advertisement. The secretary
43	gave her such an odd look that the young woman asked what
44	it the matter was. 'I don't think you quite understand,' replied the
45	secretary. 'It's you who have to pay for him £400'.

---

31	36	41 ....
32	37	42 ....
33	38	43 ....
34	39	44 ....
35	40	45 ....

In the examination, your answer on the answer sheet would look like this:

0	the	0 ▭ ▭
0	✓	0 ▭ ▭

4 For questions **46–57**, read the following notes made about a museum inspection. Use the information to complete the numbered gaps in the formal letter to the head of the museum. Then write the new words in the space provided. **Use no more than three words** for each gap. The exercise begins with an example (**0**). The words which you need **do not** occur in the notes.

Notes on visit to the
Humphrey Davy Museum of Mining Technology

Supposed to open at 10 a.m. – opened at 10.12 a.m. Why? Man who opened door mumbled insults and looked a mess. Cost £3 to get in – no ticket issued. Two exhibition rooms closed – no idea why. Two other rooms in semi-darkness. Six out of ten of the kinetic displays in the Children's Gallery did not work when the buttons were pressed. There were no labels on thirty exhibits and another ten had labels too close to the floor. The 'Ace Café' had run out of coffee and my 'Collier's Sandwich' (prawn and mayonnaise) was probably left over from the day before.

Dear Dr Crompton,
    As part of our survey of local museums, a representative of the Barchester Consumers' Group visited your museum on 21st August. We are sure that, in the interests of providing a better service to the public, you would like to receive a summary of her (**0**) ..findings..
    It seems that although you advertise an (**46**) .... of 10 a.m. there was a twelve-minute (**47**) .... and no (**48**) .... was offered by the attendant who opened the door. In fact, his (**49**) .... was rather unpleasant and his uniform could not be described as (**50**) .... Our representative also reports that no ticket was issued in return for the (**51**) .... of £3. Apparently two exhibition rooms were closed without any explanation being given and two other rooms were inadequately (**52**) .... More than (**53**) .... of the kinetic displays in the Children's Gallery were (**54**) .... Labels were (**55**) .... from thirty exhibits and ten others had labels very close to the floor. Our representative was also disappointed as coffee was (**56**) .... and she reports that the sandwich was (**57**) ....
    If you have any comments to make on our observations, we will be delighted to discuss them with you.
    Yours sincerely,
    Jane Smith

In the examination, your answer on the answer sheet would look like this:

0	findings	0

SECTION C

5 *For questions* **58–63**, *read through the following text and then choose from list* **A–J** *the best phrase or sentence given below it to fill each of the blanks. Write one letter* (**A–J**) *in the space provided.* **Some of the answers do not fit at all**. *The exercise begins with an example* (**0**).

WORLD WAR I SHELLS

Twice a day throughout the summer in a field outside the small Belgian town of Poelkapelle, a strange ritual takes place. First, a siren sounds. Then a number of boxes are lowered into specially prepared pits. (**0**) ..*J* , throwing clouds of earth into the air. (**58**) ... ; it is only another consignment of World War I shells exploding 75 years late.

Bomb disposal experts at Poelkapelle will be hard at work for many years to come. (**59**) ... , but best estimates suggest that of 1.5 billion shells fired on the Western Front between 1914 and 1918, about 30% failed to explode on impact. (**60**) ... , most of which are still out there. In the countryside around Poelkapelle, farmers plough up these deadly souvenirs almost daily. (**61**) ... ; after unearthing the shells they leave them by the roadside to be collected by an army jeep. The shells, however, remain potentially unstable and lethal as most of them are badly corroded after so many decades in the ground.

(**62**) ... . This is initially difficult because they are encrusted with rust and dirt. Officers used to clean them by hand in the open air. Now they use a high-pressure water jet or, if the dirt proves too stubborn, they remove it with a remote-control machine. (**63**) ... . Shells over 50 kg have to be exploded at sea; the remainder are stored, ready to be detonated at the ritual hours of 11.45 am and 3.30 pm.

A The local people are used to it

B It does not say much for the quality control in the munitions factories of Britain and Germany

C Only after positive identification of their country of origin can the shells be made safe

D Most of the field guns used in World War I were very inaccurate at long range

E Once cleaned and classified, the shells are placed in wooden boxes, separated by sand

F That makes 400 million unexploded shells

G These are dug out by army vehicles

H Army personnel try to identify all types of shells

I Over the years they have grown to treat them with a certain indifference

J Shortly afterwards huge explosions rock the area

In the examination, your answer on the answer sheet would look like this:

6 *You have been asked to write an article for a magazine. It is one of a series of articles entitled 'Famous Women'. Read the notes below and then use them to prepare the article. Write **no more than one sentence** for each numbered set of notes. Use connecting words and phrases as appropriate. You may add words and change the form of the words given in the notes but do not add any extra information. The first point has been expanded for you as an example (**0**).*

AMY JOHNSON

0	1904	born Hull (industrial town, NE coast England)
81	1922–25	Sheffield University (Modern Languages)
	1925–27	work in Hull (typist)
82	1927	move to London (solicitor's office)
	1928	member – London Aeroplane Club
83	1929	qualified pilot + aircraft mechanic – leaves job – concentrates on flying
84	1930	19½ day solo flight London → Australia – fame and fortune
85	1931	attempts flight to China – ends near Warsaw (Poland)
		successful flight to Tokyo (Japan)
	1932	record-breaking solo flight to Cape Town (South Africa)
86	1932	marriage to Jim Mollison – joint attempt at round-the-world flight – both survive crash (USA)
87	1934	second crash (Pakistan) during London–Australia air race → break-up of marriage?
88	1936	record-breaking solo return flight London → Cape Town
89	1941	tragic disappearance over English Channel – bad weather – no wreckage or body

In the 1930s Amy Johnson was famous as a pilot who flew long-distance routes in record time.

Example:

0 She was born in 1904 in Hull, which is an industrial town on the north-east coast of England.

81

82

83

84

85

86

87

88

89

PAPER 4 LISTENING (approximately 45 minutes)

This test requires you to listen to a selection of recorded material and answer the accompanying questions.
*There are four sections to the test, A, B, C and D. You will hear Section B **once** only. All the other parts of the test will be heard twice. During the test there will be a pause before each section to allow you to look through the questions, and other pauses to let you think about your answers.*

SECTION A

You will hear a recording of a radio sports report. Listen to the tape and complete the information in questions 1–9 below. You will need to write a number, a letter or a few words.
You will hear the recording twice.

Football results

1	England		South Korea	
2	Germany		Costa Rica	
3	Holland		USA	
4	Argentina		Austria	
5	Italy		Lithuania	

Boxing

Has a fight between Manuel Fernandez and Barry Jason definitely been arranged?   *(Write yes/no)*

6 [   ]

Golf

Who won last year's European title?

  A Philip Johnston
  B Bruce Chappell
  C Christian Bernhardt

7 [   ]

Why is Christian Bernhardt not playing in this year's competition?

8 [   ]

Tennis

How many times has Marina Stieff already won the Tournament?   **9** ▢

SECTION B

You will hear the chairperson of the Technological Society making an announcement at the end of a meeting. For questions 10–19, complete the information sheet. You will need to write a number or a few words. Listen very carefully as you will hear this piece only once.

The Technological Society

INTERNATIONAL DEPARTMENT

Course dates, fees and other expenses

Location: **10** [   ] Brimston Square

Fee includes: **11** [   ]

Extra costs: **12** [   ]

13 [   ]

Overseas participants may incur extra costs for: **14** [   ]

Industrial Relations course   **Management Today course**

Cost: **15** £ [   ]   Cost: **16** approx £ [   ]

Length of courses: **17** [   ]

Training Officers' course

Cost: £1,160 for Society members

£860 for   **18** [   ]

Length of course: **19** [   ]

SECTION C

You will hear part of a radio programme in which the interviewer is talking to a woman about a speech disorder known as 'stammering'. For questions 20–25, indicate the most appropriate response, A, B, C or D.
You will hear the piece twice.

20 What does Anita Andrews feel about being on the radio?
  A nervous
  B proud
  C grateful
  D embarrassed

21 How was she treated at school?
  A The teachers tended to be impatient.
  B Her friends refused to play with her.
  C The teachers asked her difficult questions.
  D Her friends used to imitate her.

22 How did Joseph try to stop himself from stammering?
  A by going to a speech therapist
  B by avoiding his mother's speech patterns
  C by speaking very quickly
  D by talking as little as possible

23 Why did the speech unit insist on Joseph's parents attending the course?
  A because stammering is a genetic defect
  B because his mother was also a stammerer
  C because Joseph found family life difficult
  D because stammering can be related to family behaviour

24 What did Joseph's parents learn from the course?
  A They had to believe that their son would improve.
  B They had to face up to their son's stammer.
  C They had to encourage Joseph to speak more slowly.
  D They had to become more sensitive to the needs of others.

25 Why does Anita refer to the film 'A Fish Called Wanda'?
  A because it shows how amusing a stammer can be
  B because it shows how difficult it is to cure a stammer
  C because it shows how destructive a stammer can be
  D because it shows how a stammer can be inherited

20 …

21 …

22 …

23 …

24 …

25 …

SECTION D

You will hear various people talking about the different holidays they have taken.
Task One *lists the type of holidays. Put them in the order in which you hear them by filling in the boxes numbered* **26–30** *with the appropriate letter.*
Task Two *lists the speakers' reasons for choosing a holiday. Put them in order by filling in the boxes numbered* **31–35** *with the appropriate letter.*
You will hear the recording twice.

TASK ONE

A skiing

B cruise | 26 |

C mountaineering | 27 |

D caravan

E country farm | 28 |

F diving | 29 |

G fishing | 30 |

H camping

TASK TWO

A fresh air and exercise

B family reunion | 31 |

C good climatic conditions | 32 |

D cultural interest

E peace and quiet | 33 |

F a taste of luxury | 34 |

G sun, sand and sea | 35 |

H low cost

PHASE B: HARBOUR SCENES

Set 1: Pictures (for Candidate A)

1.5C

1.5G

1.5D

1.5H

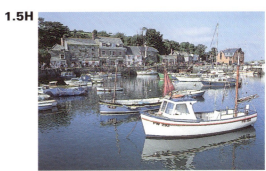

1.5E

1.5I

1.5F

1.5J

PHASE B: HARBOUR SCENES

Set 1: Pictures (for Candidate B)

1.5K

1.5O

1.5L

1.5P

1.5M

1.5Q

1.5N

1.5R

PHASE B: PAST AND PRESENT

Set of pictures (for Candidates A and B)

1.5A

1.5B

PHASE C: 'I could never...'

Set of pictures (for Candidates A and B)

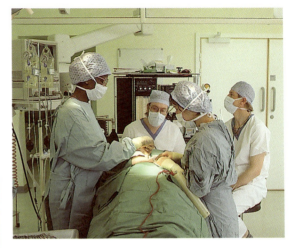
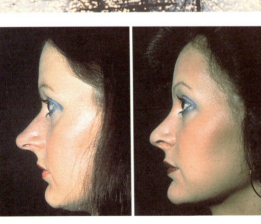

0%   100%

| I could never | I might | I'll have a go | Of course I can |

PHASE B: DIETS

Picture (for Candidates A and B)

2.5G

PHASE B: DIETS

Picture (for Candidates A and B)

2.5H

PHASE C: EDUCATION

Set of pictures (for Candidates A and B)

applying make-up

the environment

car maintenance

swimming

first aid

Mon	French	Geography	Maths	Sport	
Tues	English		History	Maths	Science
Wed	Geography	French		Cookery / Woodwork	
Thurs	History	Maths	English	Science	
Fri	Geography	Music	PE	History	Art

operating a computer

the Arts

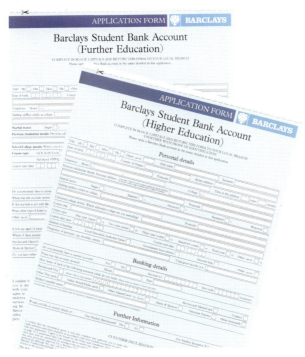

official forms

gardening

music

dancing

C9

PHASE B: HOLIDAY ACCOMMODATION

Set of pictures (for Candidates A and B)

2.5A

2.5B

2.5C

2.5D

2.5E
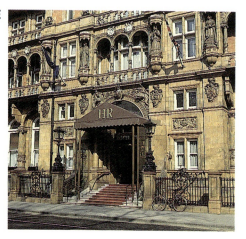

2.5E

PHASE B: A ROOM OF YOUR OWN

Picture for Candidate A

3.5A

Picture for Candidate B

3.5B

PHASE C: OLYMPIC SYMBOL

Set of pictures (for Candidates A, B and C)

PHASE C: ENVIRONMENT COMPETITION

Set of pictures (for Candidates A, B and C)

**Picture for
Candidate C**

PHASE B: LIFESTYLES AND PEOPLE

**Picture for
Candidate B**

**Picture for
Candidate A**

PAPER 5 SPEAKING (15 minutes)

There will be two examiners, one acting as an Interlocutor and one as an Assessor. You will be examined together with another candidate, referred to below as 'your partner'. One of you will be Candidate A and the other will be Candidate B.

Phase A (3 minutes)

You and your partner will talk about yourselves and each other. You will be asked to find out and offer information about you and your partner's background, interests, career plans, etc.

Phase B (3–4 minutes)

You will each be given the opportunity to talk for a minute. First you will be given the *same* set of six pictures (Holiday accommodation).
The Interlocutor will ask Candidate A to talk about the six pictures in a particular way and will explain this in full. The pictures are to be found in the centre section of this book on p. C10.
Candidate A will have one minute to speak.
Candidate B will listen carefully.
The Interlocutor will then ask Candidate B to respond to Candidate A's pictures in a particular way and will explain this in full.
Candidate B will have twenty seconds to speak.
You will then be given a further set of two pictures (Diets) on pp. C6 and C7. You will both be looking at the same two pictures. The Interlocutor will give instructions to Candidates B and A. Candidate B will talk about the pictures in a particular way for one minute. Candidate A will be allowed to respond to what has been said.

Phase C (3–4 minutes)

The Interlocutor will place a set of pictures (Education) on pp. C8 and C9 between you and your partner and will ask you to look at them together.
These pictures provide the basis for a discussion between you and your partner.
The Interlocutor will give instructions and you will have three or four minutes for this.

Phase D (3–4 minutes)

This will be based on what you have discussed in Phase C. You will first be invited to report the outcome of your discussion, saying whether you agree or not with your partner. You will then take part in a more general discussion based on what has been discussed in Phase C. Both the Interlocutor and the Assessor will take part in this discussion.

Practice Test 3

PAPER 1 READING (1 hour 15 minutes)

This paper requires you to read four texts and answer the accompanying questions.
For each question, choose one answer from the appropriate list of choices.

FIRST TEXT/QUESTIONS 1–13

Answer questions **1–13** *by referring to the newspaper article on page* **51**.

Questions **1–13**: *for which mountain or region are the following statements true,* **according to the article**? *Choose your answers from the list of mountains and regions* **(A–H)**.

Note: When more than one answer is required, these may be given **in any order**. *Some choices may be required more than once.*

Harsh weather conditions can be found there.	
1 … **2** … **3** …	
Getting there is relatively cheap.	**A** Bonnati Pillar
4 …	
No climb has been attempted there.	**B** K2
5 …	
It takes a long time to get there.	**C** The Andes
6 …	
Climbers have to deal with bureaucracy there.	**D** Mount McKinley
7 …	
People have made solo climbs there.	**E** Tienshan
8 … **9** …	
Climbers come across man-made structures there.	**F** Lhotse Middle
10 …	
Disasters continue to happen there.	**G** The Eiger
11 …	
It is not as easy to climb there as people say.	**H** Everest
12 …	
Only the best climbers make successful climbs there.	
13 …	

HIGH ADVENTURE

PLENTY of adventures are available to the climber who dares – on Everest alone, before you consider any other area of the world.

Given that ever since that historic moment at 11.30 am on May 29th 1953 when the Sherpa Tensing Norgay, GM, and Sir Edmund Hilary, KBE, became the first men to set foot on the world's highest peak, some 300 climbers have made it to the top of Everest by a variety of routes, one might be forgiven for supposing that that mountain held no more mystery and presented no more challenges. Especially when one remembers that in 1978 Rheinhold Messner and Peter Habeler did it without bottled oxygen, that in 1985 Messner became the first man to climb it alone, that Sherpa Sundare has climbed it five times, that the American Richard Bass reached the summit at the age of 55 years and 130 days, and that from 21st–30th April 1985, Arne Naess's Norwegian expedition succeeded in putting 17 people on the summit, including eight in one day.

Indeed, there is a feeling amongst mountaineers that, given sufficient resources, even the most inexperienced climber can look good on Everest. Permission is pretty easy to acquire provided one attends carefully enough to one's application and is sufficiently furnished with supplies of the hard folding stuff. (10,000 dollars should be enough to ensure an Everest booking for up to nine climbers.) And yet, no matter how many high altitude porters one may hire, or how state-of-the-art one's lightweight clothing and equipment, or how many fixed camps and ropes there may be in place on the way up, danger is always

lurking around the next ridge: especially when the weather turns. Late April to May is the best time to be in the Himalayas: before the monsoon hits.

Fortunately, there have not been any major catastrophes on Everest recently – which is more than can be said for K2. Though only two ropes' length short of Everest, this mountain could not be more different.

The Karakorams are set in the wildest imaginable landscape of range upon mountain range. Just to get one's first sight of K2 takes 12 days of hard walking from the nearest road, compared with the two days it takes from the Sherpa village of Namshe Bazaar to Everest Base Camp. And because bottled oxygen is hardly ever used on K2 (unlike Everest), it has the reputation (well-deserved) of being a real climber's mountain.

But however much the mountains of Asia may continue to seize the public imagination, for the climbers themselves there are plenty of other mountain ranges to be explored and more than enough challenges to be faced – in Russia, in South America, in Alaska, and in Europe.

The North Face of the Eiger, for example, is still considered a formidable adversary. Not only is one confronted with 9,000 feet of sheer climbing (most big Alpine faces are about 3,000 feet), but certain parts are very difficult to reverse climb in the event of bad weather. (There is an added surreal element in the shape of the doors set into the rock face which lead to the comfort and safety of the Jungfraujoch railways and which are often only inches away from the climbers' noses as they clamber past.)

There are always new routes to

be negotiated at all levels of climbing. Particularly in the Western Alps – Zermatt, the Mont Blanc Massif, the Bernese Oberland …

For those who wish to add an extra dimension of discomfort to their hardship, Mount McKinley in Alaska enjoys the distinction of being the coldest mountain in the world. The Andean peaks of Peru, Ecuador and Bolivia are blessed with some of the most reliable weather to be found anywhere, and are set amidst some of the most enchanting bird, plant and animal life imaginable. As for Russia, an increasing number of climbers are heading for the Caucasus, for the Pamirs, where there are three 7,000-metre peaks still to be climbed, and for Tienshan, where there are a further two.

Not least of the joys of climbing in Russia is the ease and lack of serious expense (100 dollars a day) with which the international Mountain Camps lay on helicopter flights to the base camps. You wouldn't get two minutes in the Alps for that!

These days, solo climbing seems to be all the rage. Everyone got very excited last summer when Catherine Destevel made a solo ascent of the Bonnati Pillar – despite the fact that Bonnati himself was alone when he first did it. But in British mountaineering circles at least, such feats are not held to be important. Not when there are still summits to be climbed, like Lhotse Middle – a fearsome ridge, 8,500 metres up on the Everest massif between Lhotse and Nuptse, so tortuous and so inaccessible that no one has yet pitted their skills against it. But they will. Everything will be climbed one day.

SECOND TEXT/QUESTIONS 14–20

*For questions **14–20**, you must choose which of the paragraphs **A–H** on page **53**
fit into the numbered gaps in the following magazine article. There is one extra
paragraph which does not fit in any of the gaps.*

BRINGING UP BADGERS

'What now?' was my immediate thought, as one of my helpers carried a cardboard box towards me. Since my husband Derek and I turned our dairy farm in Somerset into an 'open farm' six years ago, we've established a reputation for looking after orphaned animals. But the noise coming from the box – a cross between a cackle and a bark – was not one I recognised, so it was with great interest that I peered in to see three small grey badger cubs, each no more than eight inches long. Their coats (later to reveal fleas) were like velvet, and milky-coloured eyes looked up at me from three tiny black-and-white striped heads.

14

I could see they were healthy and well but they were cold and whimpering. After defleaing them, I took them into the farmhouse kitchen and installed them beside the stove for warmth. There were two females, Primrose and Bluebell, and a male, Willow. Initially I used a syringe to feed them but each cub had to be wiped with a warm cloth first to simulate the sensation of the mother licking them. This encouraged them to empty their bowels and bladder. For the first two or three days they were fed every four hours.

15

The vet's post mortem revealed that Willow had died from a lung infection. When bottle feeding any animal it is important not to let it drink too fast, as liquid can overflow into the lungs. In Willow's case this had caused an infection that would have been difficult to rectify, even with the help of antibiotics, in one so small.

16

Willow II joined the fold. At six weeks, he was about two weeks younger than the females and over the next few days I discovered why his mother had left him. Never had anything been so difficult to feed. To place the bottle's teat in his mouth and cajole him into drinking I had to keep moving it around and squeezing it. After a full 10 minutes he would latch on to it as if he had not drunk all day. By the end of April the females were weaned onto creamed rice and then literally anything. It was to be a different story for Willow. He was happy to give up the bottle but could not master the habit of eating without walking through his food, tipping it over or just sitting in it. Eventually I offered him a sausage, which little by little was chewed, played with and finally eaten. After a week of sausages he was ready to move on to something else.

17

By August my foundlings had begun to turn nocturnal and would go for walks only at dusk or late at night. We often went through the cider orchard; in its long grass, everyone was fair game. The cubs would get excited, ruffle up their fur so that they looked like snowballs and chase each other's tails. As 'human badgers' we were included in this sport. I learnt to avoid those playful charges that ended with a sharp nip, but Derek accompanied us only occasionally and so never grasped this skill: his reactions to being 'caught' were sometimes as colourful as his bruises.

18

The local press took some pictures of me walking the badgers, and such was the response that we started an appeal to build a sett on the farm for the badgers to move into. With advice freely given, we designed our badgers' new home. Daniel, one of our sons, drew up the plans and we built a sett complete with tunnels, an enclosure and a badger gate facing the same way as their nightly walks.

19

The cost of the building work was far more than we envisaged but a local bus company (the aptly named Badgerline) sponsored part of the appeal, and local firms donated building materials. Everyone, it seemed, wanted to see the badgers with a home of their own.

| 20 |

These days my walks with them are not as regular, especially as they are not fully awake until midnight. We see Primrose only occasionally (she has joined a neighbouring sett) but Bluebell and Willow II still rush up to say hello before they go dashing off into the night. This is their territory now, an area that they have come to know well and a home they have readily accepted.

A At nearly five months old, they were all eating cereals for breakfast; a meat and vegetable meal for lunch and fruit and nuts, cheese, hard-boiled eggs and sunflower seeds in the evening. The usual diet for badgers is 60 per cent earthworms, plus beetles and bugs, baby rabbits, mice and voles and even shoots or roots of plants. Certainly my badgers were much better off than other cubs that year; the summer was exceptionally hot and digging for earthworms must have been almost impossible.

B Disheartened by my failure, I continued rearing the others. But fate works in strange ways: six days later a local farmer, who had heard about our cubs, came to see me. Behind some silage bags he had discovered a single male cub, abandoned by its mother. He knew she would not return; the area had been disturbed too much and already the cub was cold and hungry.

C I had never seen badger cubs before. As most of them are born between mid-January and mid-March, they usually spend their early life underground and, if orphaned, die of starvation, never to be found. These three had been brought in by building contractors; while laying drain pipes, their machinery had bored into the sett before they realised it. The mother was found dead with her babies still suckling her.

D This didn't happen with the females, but poor Willow was true to form. Before long, apart from his definite striped head, we had a totally bald badger. He was healthy, but because badgers tug on each other's skin in play, games proved rather painful.

E Within a week the cubs had progressed to drinking from a bottle and were moving around, albeit shakily. With each other for company and a heated pad as a substitute 'mum', they seemed very contented. Three weeks after their arrival, however, I noticed that Willow seemed lethargic, although he was still taking food as normal. It was a warning sign. I should have reacted straightaway; not realising its importance, I awoke the next morning to find him dead.

F It had three chambers, one slightly larger than the others, with a glass side to enable people to see into the sett from a darkened enclosure. As the sett began to take shape, the badgers would explore it before going on their walks. Eventually walks were forgotten in the excitement of climbing through the tunnels and sorting out bedding.

G Early one evening they finally moved in. After watching them for a while, we left them to settle. Half an hour later I crept back to see if all was well, to be met with the sight of three badgers curled up in their chambers sound asleep.

H It was during two of these late-night walks in the very dry period that I spotted other badgers in our field. Presumably they were having to extend their territories to find enough food, although badgers are very territorial and will kill others that wander into their territory. We were even warned that they would climb into our badger pen and kill the cubs, so sheet metal was placed over the gate to make it as inaccessible as possible.

THIRD TEXT/QUESTIONS 21–25

Read the following article from a magazine and answer questions **21–25** *on page* **55**. *Indicate the letter* **A**, **B**, **C** *or* **D** *against the number of each question,* **21–25**. *Give only one answer to each question.*

Blacksmiths

THROUGHOUT the ages, iron has exerted a powerful pull on the human imagination, and the men who work it have often been regarded as much more than skilled craftsmen. Before the Industrial Revolution, blacksmiths enjoyed the same status as doctors and astrologers, because they were the sole providers of weapons, armour and farming tools.

They have also been fêted as artists. Eighteenth-century smiths produced the wonderfully baroque ironwork for St Paul's Cathedral. The sinuous metalwork of French and Belgian Art Nouveau architecture was always the work of a talented blacksmith.

But practitioners of these ancient skills had become almost extinct in Britain by the late 1960s, for heavy industry had ceased to have any use for them, and tower-block architects rarely used anything as graceful and pleasing as a wrought-iron handrail.

Over the past 10 years, however, there has been something of a revival – thanks to greater interest in decorative architecture and a less conservative approach to interior design. Even so, much of the work looks surprisingly clichéd: manufacturers of gates and balconies still advertise their wares as 'classical' or 'Victorian-

style'. You can't walk into a trendy design store without being assailed by rusty candlesticks with dangly bits.

Thankfully, alternatives exist and a series of events over the next few weeks aims to promote the blacksmith's craft. The first of these, an exhibition of forged ironwork by members of the British Artist Blacksmiths Association (BABA), opened last week at the Fire & Iron gallery in Leatherhead, Surrey.

Alan Dawson, the secretary of BABA, says: 'We could be at the start of a new Iron Age, because, in a sense, both the general public and blacksmiths have had their blinkers removed.' Power tools have liberated smiths from all that labouring over a hot anvil, and they can now bend, split, twist and spot-weld the metal with relative ease. 'In short,' says Dawson, 'these artists now have a material which allows them to express themselves.'

About 250 pieces have been produced for the show, ranging from bookends to a spiral staircase. Reserve prices start at £90 and climb well into four figures. Most of the money raised will go to individual makers, 'but a percentage of every sale will be retained by the Association for the promotion of good ironwork,' says Dawson.

His own contributions consist of an eight-foot gate, and a standard lamp topped with a mouth-blown glass shade.

'My style results from just allowing steel to bend and flow into shape when it's hot. It's a bit like drawing with metal in space,' he says.

Many of the artists admit to being fascinated by iron. Unlike most metals, which are relatively malleable when cold, iron and steel are a tougher, more demanding medium. Susan May, a jeweller by training, says, 'It's quite magical, because it's incredibly soft when it's hot, but as soon as it cools down, it becomes really rigid and immovable again.'

Ann Catrin Evans' mild steel door-knockers and handles seem to have been inspired by those bleak castles that are a stock feature of horror films. One of her designs is shaped like a ball and chain, another like a Celtic cross. 'I love the fact that steel is cold and hard,' she says. 'And the way it feels as though it's there forever.'

No other base metal can have given man as much visual pleasure, or a greater feeling of security. The chances of iron being used decoratively for the next thousand years are good, to say the least – as long as we don't have to look at any more rusty candlesticks, that is.

21 Interest in blacksmiths' work has revived because
    A they have developed a number of new skills.
    B people have started to want variety in design.
    C gates and balconies have come back into fashion.
    D they now produce better-quality products.

22 What is the aim of the BABA exhibition?
    A To demonstrate the modern blacksmith at work.
    B To encourage people to become blacksmiths.
    C To promote the tools available to blacksmiths.
    D To show what modern blacksmiths can produce.

23 Some of the profits from the show will be used
    A to start an association of blacksmiths.
    B to purchase good materials for blacksmiths to use.
    C to publicise high-quality goods made by blacksmiths.
    D to run training courses for blacksmiths.

24 Susan May likes using iron because
    A it is perfect for making jewellery.
    B it can easily be shaped when cold.
    C it is challenging to work with.
    D it becomes cool very quickly.

25 Which of the following statements best expresses the writer's view?
    A The art of decorative ironwork is likely to survive.
    B The revival of interest in blacksmiths will be short-lived.
    C Old-fashioned ironwork will come back into fashion.
    D Blacksmiths are unfortunately a thing of the past.

21 ...

22 ...

23 ...

24 ...

25 ...

FOURTH TEXT/QUESTIONS 26–41

Answer questions **26–41** *by referring to the newspaper article* **below** *and on page* **57**.

Questions **26–32**. *According to the article, which goods are sold using the methods on the left below? Choose your answers from the list of goods* (**A–H**) *on the right below.*
Note: When more than one answer is required, these may be given **in any order**
Some choices may be required more than once.

placing goods next to items they go together with	**A** washing powders
26	**B** tea
dispersing goods around the store	**C** vegetables
27 .... **28**	**D** salad dressing
displaying the goods in small quantities only	**E** dairy products
29	**F** bread
having the goods appropriately lit	**G** ready-made meals
30 .... **31**	**H** clothes
making sure these goods are the first things people see	
32	

Questions **33–41**. *In which sections* (**A–I**) *of the article are the following mentioned?*
Note: When more than one answer is required, these may be given **in any order**.
Some choices may be required more than once.

crime prevention	**33**............		
interior decoration	**34**	**35**	**36** ....
customers who always buy the same brands	**37**		
goods that are not profit-making	**38**		
customers' movements around the store	**39**............	**40**	**41** ....

TALKING SHOP

Ever entered a store and come away with more than you intended to buy? We reveal the selling devices shops use that are designed to make you spend, spend, spend.

A The image of freshness
Supermarkets know from their market research that shoppers place a premium on fresh produce being in stores. They may place their fruit and veg at the entrance of a store, or even a display of house plants for sale, to enhance this. They may also provide an in-store bakery that wafts irresistible fresh bread smells around a large area of the store. The colour of the store's fixtures may heighten the image, too – for example, green may be

used because of its association with fresh produce. The bulk of what supermarkets sell – pre-packaged grocery items such as frozen foods and washing powders – may be quite different from this image.

B Displaying to advantage

The location of products in the store is considered all-important in determining how well a particular brand sells. Nowhere is this more developed than in supermarkets. With computerised stock-control, supermarkets can find out the parts of the store from which shoppers will select items most often. In these areas can be found products with the highest mark-ups or ones which, though less profitable, sell very quickly. Traditionally in retailing, 'eye-level' means 'buy-level' – shelves at eye height are eagerly sought by manufacturers, or may be reserved for certain own-brand items. 'Dump bins' containing special offers tempt those who find it hard to resist a bargain. Increasingly popular is 'complementation' – placing dessert or salad dressings, say, over units containing ice-creams or items that may be eaten with salads such as burgers.

C Spreading staples around the store

Supermarkets may spread low-price staples such as bread, tea and sugar around their stores and a long way from the entrance – shoppers have to pass tempting, higher-profit lines on the way. In similar vein, chainstores may locate the products they have a good reputation for as far away from the store entrance as possible. They can rely on a degree of customer loyalty towards these products, so they gamble that shoppers will go actively looking for them around the store, passing other wares that might tempt them.

D Less sells more

Chainstores have transformed the presentation of their wares in recent years. Much of the pioneering work has been done by the *Next* chain, which turned away from the 'pile them high, sell them cheap' approach to popular fashion. *Next* stores have a 'boutique' appeal – they're noted for displaying limited fashion-wear on the shelves, giving the impression that the merchandise is exclusive. Of course, *Next*'s clothing is not less mass-produced than that of their rivals – the company's success is as much a testament to good store design as it is to well-designed clothing.

E Tempting totals

Food shoppers, it seems, are more responsive to the overall size of their weekly or fortnightly bill than to the prices of individual items. Supermarkets take advantage of this by stocking a mix of low mark-up staples and high mark-up items, so it shouldn't be assumed everything that a supermarket sells is cheap. Low prices are of direct appeal to the thrifty shopper. It's often said that supermarkets deliberately lose money on certain staples to draw shoppers in – known as 'loss leaders'. More commonly, their low prices are achieved by buying in huge quantities from manufacturers, by offering them a prominent place to display their products or by exceeding sales targets – all of which attract big discounts from the manufacturers.

F The all-important price-tag

Shoppers tend to buy fewer items in chainstores and may be more aware of individual pricing as a result. So the importance of pricing, say, a blouse at £14.99 as opposed to £15, still holds. (It's also a useful device, apparently, to reduce theft among the shop's own staff, who are

obliged to ring up a sale in order to give the penny change.)

G Lighting to effect

Both supermarkets and chainstores give careful thought to lighting. With chainstores, the aim is to achieve lighting which is as close to natural light as possible so that shoppers get a fair idea of what the colour of the clothes will be like in daylight. With supermarkets, special lighting (and mirrors) may be used to enhance certain foods, particularly fresh fruit and veg.

H Walk this way

Many chainstores have divided up their floors with different carpeting – one pattern for the routes through a store and one defining sales areas. Shoppers are drawn naturally along these routes – known within the trade as the 'Yellow Brick Road'. It's not always successful – some shoppers are reluctant to stray off the routes into the sales areas. *Marks and Spencer*, for example, use wood or marble covering for routes, encouraging shoppers to walk on to the more welcoming carpet in sales areas.

I In-store promotion

As you enter a supermarket, giant colour photographs of succulent roasts, fancy cakes and cheeses hit you – irresistible if you've had nothing to eat before setting out on your shopping trip. In the United States, 'video trolleys' are being tried out in a number of supermarkets. Each trolley has a screen which advertises products as you shop. Sensors at the end of shelves trigger relevant advertising – so the shopper passing the cook-chill cabinets, say, may receive an ad. on the screen for ready-made moussaka. Such trolleys are aimed unashamedly at the impulse shopper, and the makers claim they increase sales by around 30 per cent.

PAPER 2 WRITING (2 hours)

This paper contains one Section A task and four Section B tasks. You must complete the Section A task and **one** *from Section B, using an appropriate style for each task.*
The two sections carry equal marks.
Read the task instructions and consider the information **carefully** *both for Section A and the task which you select for Section B.*

SECTION·A

1 Last month you spent a week in England for High Life Travel as an interpreter for a group of tourists from your country. Unfortunately you and many members of the group were unhappy with the programme. High Life Travel has invited you to take part again as an interpreter but you feel that the conditions should be improved.

Read the advertisement for the holiday, an extract from a recent letter from a friend and, on page **59**, *the programme with your notes based on the week when you were working.*
Then, **using the information carefully**, *write a letter to High Life Travel* **accepting** *the job but* **suggesting** *how the week's programme and your conditions of employment should be improved. Your letter should be about* **250** *words and should include addresses.*

Holiday of your Dreams

✳ a week in England in a luxury hotel ✳
✳ famous London sights ✳
✳ excursions out of London ✳
✳ excellent value ✳

For more information, contact:
High Life Travel
4 Seed Street
London SW1Y 4BZ
Tel: 0171 384 1727

I can't believe what you told me about your job – to think that more than half the people were ready to go home by the third day! It hardly seems fair considering what it cost. Also, paying you so little (although, as you say, you weren't a professional interpreter) AND then not paying your expenses – I'd think twice about working for them again!

'HIGH LIFE' PROGRAMME

DAY 1   1430   Arrive London Heathrow

            1530   Transfer to Hotel Royal, Piccadilly.

                      Evening free

first night in a strange city

dirty, no lift or room service, rooms on 4th floor

DAY 2   0900   Visit Royal London & Art Gallery

            1300   Lunch in a typical English restaurant

a hamburger restaurant!

            1930   See one of London's musicals

back row in gallery – couldn't see

cancelled because of bad weather – nothing to do

DAY 3   0900   Boat trip on River Thames

            1430   Guided walk through City of London

            2000   Bus tour — London by Night

bus broke down – 2 hours wasted

?!

DAY 4   0900   (Day) trip to Stratford on Avon: Shakespeare's birthplace

            2030   Visit London's top discotheque

no time to see anything!

DAY 5   0900   Day trip to the famous university town, Cambridge

                      Evening free

no guide provided

DAY 6   0900   Guided walk through 3 London parks

                      Afternoon free for shopping —— *more free time!*

            2000   Evening at the Opera

DAY 7   0930   Leave Hotel Royal

thank goodness!

            1230   Depart London Heathrow

SECTION B

*Choose **one** of the following writing tasks. Your answer should follow exactly the instructions given.*
*Write approximately **250** words.*

2

> Do you use English at college or at work? The *English-users Newsletter* would like to hear from you about any problems you have experienced when using English and any benefits you have gained. We're sure you've got some interesting things to say to people in situations similar to yours, and we're keen to publish articles with as many different viewpoints as possible.

Write an **article** for the newsletter and share your views with people in a similar situation.

3 In a London museum there is to be an exhibition of some items of great interest from your country, and you have been asked to assist with the publicity. Write a **leaflet** which outlines the history of the items and explains their importance within and outside your country.

4 An international English language magazine is preparing an article comparing attitudes to the changing role of women in different parts of the world at the end of the twentieth century, and you have been asked to write about the subject with specific reference to the situation in your own country. Write your **contribution to the article**, focusing on one or more of the following areas: the workplace and careers; marriage and relationships; housework; politics; education.

5 Someone in your community whom you have known for a long time wants to spend a year looking after children in an English-speaking family, and has asked you to write a character reference. You should write a detailed **reference**, indicating how long and in what capacity you have known this person, the strengths and weaknesses of their personality, and why you would support their application.

PAPER 3 ENGLISH IN USE (1 hour 30 minutes)

This paper requires you to complete six tasks.
Answer all questions.
The total number of questions for tasks 1 to 5 is 62; the last task is numbered 81–89.

SECTION A

1   *For questions **1–15**, read the text below and then decide which word on page **62** best fits each space. Circle the letter you choose for each question. The exercise begins with an example (**0**).*

BECOMING A TRANSLATOR

The role of the translator in enabling literature to pass beyond its natural frontiers is receiving growing recognition. In (**0**) ... of the general increase in this (**1**) ... , it is not surprising that many people with literary interests and a knowledge of languages should think of adopting translating as a full- or part-time (**2**) ... . Some advice may usefully be (**3**) ... to such would-be translators.

The first difficulty the beginner will (**4**) ... is the unwillingness of publishers to entrust a translation to anyone who has not already (**5**) ... a reputation for sound work. The least publishers will (**6**) ... before commissioning a translation is a fairly lengthy (**7**) ... of the applicant's work, even if unpublished. Perhaps the best way the would-be translator can begin is to select some book of the type which he or she feels competent and (**8**) ... to translate, translate a (**9**) ... section of the book and then submit the book and the translation to a (**10**) ... publisher. If he or she is extremely lucky, this may (**11**) ... in a commission to translate the book. More (**12**) ... , however, publishers will (**13**) ... the book as such but if they are favourably (**14**) ... by the translation, they may very possibly commission some other book of a (**15**) ... nature which they already have in mind.

0	**A**	regard	Ⓑ	view	**C**	awareness	**D**	consideration

1	**A**	field	**B**	category	**C**	ground	**D**	class
2	**A**	work	**B**	employment	**C**	occupation	**D**	line
3	**A**	made	**B**	given	**C**	told	**D**	shown
4	**A**	encounter	**B**	involve	**C**	reveal	**D**	introduce
5	**A**	formed	**B**	set	**C**	founded	**D**	established
6	**A**	instruct	**B**	oblige	**C**	demand	**D**	direct
7	**A**	instance	**B**	case	**C**	specimen	**D**	model
8	**A**	eager	**B**	nervous	**C**	agitated	**D**	excited
9	**A**	substantial	**B**	main	**C**	grand	**D**	plentiful
10	**A**	fit	**B**	right	**C**	convenient	**D**	suitable
11	**A**	finish	**B**	lead	**C**	effect	**D**	result
12	**A**	surely	**B**	probably	**C**	certainly	**D**	expectedly
13	**A**	exclude	**B**	reject	**C**	object	**D**	disapprove
14	**A**	impressed	**B**	convinced	**C**	affected	**D**	taken
15	**A**	common	**B**	same	**C**	similar	**D**	joint

In the examination, your answer on the answer sheet would look like this:

0	B		0
			▭ ▭

2 *For questions* **16–30**, *complete the following article by writing each missing word in the space provided.* **Use only one word for each space.** *The exercise begins with an example* (**0**).

A START IN SAILING

Ask any sports enthusiast to name the most popular sports and the stock answer will probably be football, cricket, golf and rugby. A lot of people (**0**) ......*do*....... play those games but far (**16**) .... go fishing, play badminton or sail. Why do we get it wrong? Because sports editors, of newspapers and television channels, are stuck (**17**) .... their traditional patterns of judging by crowds (**18**) .... than by how many actually go out and do the thing. Sailing probably suffers most (**19**) .... this narrow-mindedness (**20**) .... it is often difficult to report and almost impossible to film except (**21**) .... huge expense.

    Yet, despite the absence of the oxygen of publicity, sailing is (**22**) .... of the most popular participant sports. Why is it so popular in Britain? Possibly because of the great island tradition of (**23**) .... a nation of sailors, but probably much more because of (**24**) .... many opportunities. Nowhere in Britain is all that far from the sea and (**25**) .... are plenty of rivers and lakes where it is easy to get afloat. But many would-be sailors are discouraged (**26**) .... taking the first steps. They worry (**27**) .... the cost of a boat, the need for special equipment, the dangers of tackling the elemental forces of nature and believe that sailing-club people (**28**) .... snobbish and unapproachable. All misconceptions. You can start sailing (**29**) .... next to nothing and find friendly sailing clubs throughout the country (**30**) .... nobody is snobbish or looks down on beginners.

In the examination, your answer on the answer sheet would look like this:

0	*do*		0
			▭ ▭

3   In **most** lines of the following text, there is either a spelling or a punctuation
    error. For each numbered line **31–43**, write the correctly spelled word(s) or
    show the correct punctuation in the spaces on your answer sheet. Some
    lines are correct. Indicate these lines with a tick (✓) in the box. The exercise
    begins with three examples (**0**).

COSTUME JEWELLERY

0	It may seem a little ridiculous to think, that people deliberately buy
0	imitations but that is most definately true of costume jewellery from
0	the 1930s which now sells for hundreds of pounds and is increasingly
31	popular in America and Europe The term 'costume jewellery' is
32	relatively new but such jewellery has been around ever since man
33	first decorated himself with bones and shells. The Romans, in
34	particular took delight in making imitation jewels from glass and
35	ceramics and combining them with preciuos stones and metal. The
36	eighteenth century saw an improvment with the arrival of hand-cut
37	glass, now referred to as paste'. This became so fashionable and
38	sought after that it rivalled diamonds both in demand and prize. Good
39	pieces of eighteenth-century paste jewellery still sell for hundreds
40	and sometimes even thousands of pounds. The real revolution in
41	costume jewellery is attributed to french designer Coco Chanel, who
42	turned it away from pure imitation off previous designs in favour
43	of 'jewels' made to be valued in their own right. Plastics were used to
	produce shapes and colours never seen before, let alone worn.

31	....	**36**	....	**41**	....
32	....	**37**	....	**42**	....
33	....	**38**	....	**43**	....
34	....	**39**	....		
35	....	**40**	....		

In the examination, your answers on the answer sheet would look like this:

0	think that	0 ▭ ▭
0	*definitely*	0 ▭ ▭
0	✓	0 ▭ ▭

4 For questions **44–55**, read the following informal note and use the information in it to complete the numbered gaps in the more formal letter. **Use not more than two words for each gap.** Then write the new words in the space. The exercise begins with an example (**0**). The words which you need **do not** occur in the informal note.

INFORMAL NOTE

> I've been asked to write a reference for Faith Good. Do you think you could help me with it? It's quite hard to know how to write a diplomatic reference for her as she isn't exactly the ideal employee. Mind you, she means well and I'd like to help her get a good job. She passed her typing and shorthand course after all and I think she's good at speaking to people over the phone. She's not bad at Spanish and she passed her driving test last month, I believe. She's a fitness fanatic and she always wears the latest fashions. She's always cracking jokes – even if some of them are pretty terrible – and she certainly doesn't worry in the slightest about talking to new people. So she fits the bill as far as the job is concerned in quite a few ways. I guess I can't avoid mentioning her appalling spelling and the way she's late for everything. But I'll finish by saying – and I think this is true really – that we'd be sorry to see her go if another company gave her a job somewhere else.

FORMAL LETTER

> Dear Mr Brown,
>   (**0**) <u>As requested</u> I am sending you a reference for Ms Faith Good. I am happy to recommend her for the position you have advertised. She has a (**44**) .... typing and shorthand and she has a good telephone (**45**) .... She speaks Spanish (**46**) .... and she holds a (**47**) .... Faith is (**48**) .... aerobics and running and she always dresses (**49**) .... She has a (**50**) .... of humour and is (**51**) .... about meeting new people. She is certainly, therefore, in many ways (**52**) .... the job that you are advertising. Although her spelling could (**53**) .... and she tends not to be (**54**) ...., we should sincerely miss her many qualities if she were to accept (**55**) .... of employment elsewhere.
>   Yours sincerely,
>   *Jenny Smith*

In the examination, your answer on the answer sheet would look like this:

0	As requested	0

SECTION C

5   *For questions* **56–60** *read through the following text and then choose from list* **A–J** *the best phrase or sentence given below it to fill each of the blanks. Write one letter* (**A–J**) *in the correct box on your answer sheet.* **Some of the suggested answers do not fit at all***. The exercise begins with an example* (**0**).

CHILDREN AND FAILURE

My seventeen-month-old niece caught sight of my ball-point pen the other day and reached out for it. It has a plastic cap that fits over the point. (**0**) J.. . After looking it over, she put it back on. Then off again; then on again. (**56**) ... . Now if I want to be able to use my pen, I have to keep it out of sight, for when she sees it, she wants to play with it. She is so deft at putting it back on that it makes me wonder about all I've read about lack of coordination in infants. (**57**) ... . These quiet summer days I spend many hours watching this baby. What comes across most vividly is that she is a kind of scientist. (**58**) ... Most of her waking time she is intensely and purposefully active, soaking up experience and trying to make sense of it, trying to find how things around her behave and trying to make them behave as she wants them to.

In the face of what looks like unbroken failure she is so persistent. (**59**) ... . But she goes right on, not the least daunted. Perhaps this is because she has not yet learnt to feel ashamed of her failures. Even a five-year-old is often embarrassed by mistakes, let alone an adult, but she is not. (**60**) ... .

A   We are always trying to distract her from dangerous experiments
B   It is a difficult job, even for an adult
C   Unlike her elders, she is not concerned with protecting herself
D   She is always observing and experimenting
E   It was a great surprise to everyone
F   A good game
G   Most of her experiments don't work
H   They may be much more skilful than we think
I   There is nothing she will not meddle with
J   She took hold of it, and after some pushing and pulling, got the cap off

In the examination, your answer on the answer sheet would look like this:

6 Use the following notes to prepare a short article for a reference book about an African mammal, the hippopotamus. Write **one sentence only** for each numbered set of notes, using connecting words and phrases as appropriate. You may add words and change the form of the words given in the notes but do not add any extra information. The first point has been expanded for you as an example (**0**).

Hippopotamus

0	_Habitat:_	mainly national parks S of Sahara
81	_Feeding:_	night on land (largely grass), day in water;
82	_Shape:_	barrel-like body; massive head; short legs — 4 toes each foot;
83	_Colour:_	mainly copper-brown; varies v. dark above — pink below
84	_Teeth:_	enlarged lower, continuously growing; only for fighting
85	_Length:_	average adult male 3.6 m nose–tail; fem. 15 cm shorter
86	_Weight:_	mature adults 1400–1600 kg
87	_Reproduction:_	mating in water; 8 months later calf born — about 50 kg
88	_Social organisation:_	hippo groups (10–100 animals), mainly fem. and young
89	_Behaviour:_	territorial fights common, usually start in/near water

Example: 0 Hippos are found mainly in national parks south of the Sahara.

81

82

83

84

85

86

87

88

89

PAPER 4 LISTENING   (approximately 45 minutes)

This paper requires you to listen to a selection of recorded material and answer the accompanying questions.
There are four sections to the test, **A, B, C** *and* **D***. You will hear Section B* **once** *only. All the other parts of the test will be heard twice. During the test there will be a pause before each section to allow you to look through the questions, and other pauses to let you think about your answers.*

SECTION A

You will hear a recording of an interview with Edward Munns, a representative from the Lighting Industry Federation. He is talking about a new type of environmentally-friendly lightbulb. Listen to what he says and complete the information for items **1–8***.*
You will hear the recording twice.

Comparison of standard lightbulb with new type:				
	Ordinary standard bulb		*Environmentally-friendly bulb*	
Expected life in number of hours		**1**		
Expected life in years if used 3 hours/day		**2**		**3**
Average cost				**4**
Current sales in UK		**5**		**6**
Probable supplier				**7**
Possible saving on electricity costs				**8**

SECTION B

*Look at the plan of Bankeira, an archaeological site. You will hear a tour guide conducting a party of visitors around the site. Listen to the recording and for questions **9–18** fill in the name of each building in the appropriate space. Listen very carefully as you will hear this piece only **once**.*

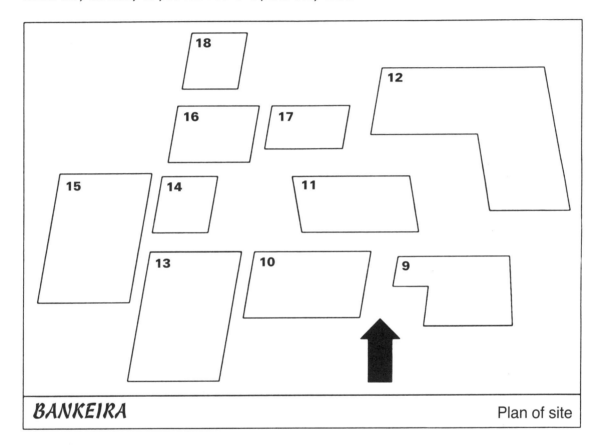

BANKEIRA   Plan of site

SECTION C

You will hear part of a radio interview with the actress Susan Davenant who is starring in a successful TV series called 'The Falling Leaves'. For questions 19–23, choose the correct option from A, B, C or D.
You will hear the piece twice.

19 Why did Susan enjoy making the series?
  A It was a success.
  B Everything went right.
  C She knew everybody.
  D Everyone got on well.

20 What made Susan walk off the set?
  A She disliked repeating the scene.
  B Her colleagues were angry with her.
  C The director criticised her acting.
  D She lost patience with herself.

21 Why did she make an effort to put on weight?
  A She was afraid of losing the part.
  B Some special costumes did not fit her.
  C She felt it would help her play the part.
  D She did not like her appearance.

22 How does she feel about being recognised by fans?
  A She feels rather annoyed.
  B She still finds it embarrassing.
  C She feels it is an invasion of privacy.
  D She accepts it as part of being well-known.

23 What is Susan's ambition?
  A To become famous for her work in theatre.
  B To direct a classical stage play.
  C To act in as many films as possible.
  D To develop her part in 'The Falling Leaves'.

SECTION D

Altogether, you will hear five short extracts, in which various people are talking about food.

TASK ONE

For questions **24–28**, match the extracts which you hear with the people listed **A–H**. For example, if you think the first extract is spoken by a chef, write **C** in box **24**.

A	Dietary expert	**24**	
B	Food manufacturer		
C	Chef	**25**	
D	Customer in restaurant	**26**	
E	Parent		
F	Neighbour	**27**	
G	Restaurant critic		
H	Guest at dinner	**28**	

TASK TWO

For questions **29–33**, match the extracts with each speaker's intention, listed **A–H**. For example, if you think the first speaker is recommending types of food, write **D** in box **29**.
You will hear the recording twice.

A	giving advice on cooking	**29**	
B	warning		
C	criticising	**30**	
D	recommending types of food	**31**	
E	praising		
F	trying to persuade	**32**	
G	expressing disgust		
H	giving advice on slimming	**33**	

PAPER 5 SPEAKING (15 minutes)

There will be two examiners, one acting as an Interlocutor and one as an Assessor. You will be examined together with another candidate refered to below as 'your partner'. One of you will be Candidate A, the second will be Candidate B.

Phase A (approximately 3 minutes)

You and your partner will talk about yourselves and each other. You will be asked to find out and offer information about you and your partners' background, interests, career plans, etc.

Phase B (approximately 3–4 minutes)

You will each be given the opportunity to talk for a minute.
You will each be given a different picture to look at (A room of your own) and you will be asked to talk about it in a particular way. The Interlocutor will explain this in full. You will be asked to show your picture to your partner while you are talking about it and your partner will be asked to listen carefully to what is being said. The pictures are to be found in the centre section of this book on pp. C11 and C12.
Candidate A will be given a picture first and will have one minute to talk.
Candidate B will then be given a different picture and will have one minute to talk.
You will then be asked to look at each other's pictures again and say whether or not you agree with what you have each said. You will have one minute to talk together.

Phase C (3–4 minutes)

The Interlocutor will place a new set of pictures (Olympic symbol) on p. C13 between you and your partner and will ask you to look at them together.
These pictures provide the basis for a discussion between you and your partner. The Interlocutor will give instructions and you will have three or four minutes for this.

Phase D (3–4 minutes)

This is based on what you have discussed in Phase C. You will first be invited to report the outcome of your discussion saying whether you agree or not with your partners. You will then take part in a more general discussion based on what has been discussed in Phase C. Both the Interlocutor and the Assessor will take part in this discussion.

Practice Test 4

PAPER 1 READING (1 hour 15 minutes)

This paper requires you to read four texts and answer the accompanying questions. For each question, choose one answer from the appropriate list of choices.

FIRST TEXT/QUESTIONS 1–17

*Answer questions **1–17** by referring to the newspaper article on page **74**.*
*For questions **1–17**, answer by choosing from sections **A–E** printed on page **75**.*
*Note: when more than one answer is required, these may be given **in any order**. Some choices may be required more than once.*

Which father or fathers

tries to avoid physical punishment?	**1**	....		
initially resented the restrictions of fatherhood?	**2**	....		
made a conscious decision to have a child?	**3**	....		
arranged his accommodation to be near his children?	**4**	....		
is involved in the children's daily routine?	**5**	....		
altered his professional duties to take account of his children?	**6**	....		
share interests with their children?	**7**	....	**8**	....
appreciated his children more as they grew older?	**9**	....		
treated his children as if they were grown up?	**10**	....		
doesn't force his children to maintain contact with him?	**11**	....		
was not as strict as his children would have wished?	**12**	....		
found his children's interests helped him with his job?	**13**	....		
had their children close together?	**14**	....	**15**	....
would have liked to attend more school events?	**16**	........;		
did not want to repeat his parents' mistakes?	**17**	....		

FROM HERE TO PATERNITY

A The theatre director

'Because of my bizarre personal life, which I cannot be proud of, I have been blessed with 35 years of small children and I can honestly say I have loved every minute. I had the pleasure of feeding the baby this morning and that for me is what being a father is all about.

'I'm terribly lucky with my children. We all love the same things: opera, theatre, books, music. It creates a great bond, especially now that they are mostly grown up and I have become a friend rather than a father.

'I don't believe in physical violence. I have been guilty of slapping my children in anger, but I don't condone it. I'm sure I have not been a deeply attentive father but I have always tried to be available. I'm here if they need me, always on the basis that they ring me. As soon as you start chasing them to ask why they have not been in touch, you impose this terrible burden of guilt. My parents did it to me and I would never do it to my children.'

B The advertising executive

'I was young when they were born, only around 25, and I admit I found the responsibilities and limitations quite irksome. It aged me quickly, but at the same time it kept me young, which is something I have always valued.

'As they became teenagers, they introduced me to things I could have drifted away from: music, youth culture, clothes. In a funny way that has been invaluable as far as running the agency has been concerned. I have never felt out of touch.

'Because I was struggling to establish the business when they were young there were things I missed: first concerts, sports days. I'm sad about that, but there are compensations now, like being able to take them on holidays to the south of France.

'They get on well with a lot of our friends and they come to parties with us and advertising awards ceremonies without feeling intimidated. I think it has been an advantage that I do something they see as glamorous and interesting.'

C The politician

'My first child was born just as I was about to be elected onto the Greater London Council, and the others followed in quite quick succession. My wife and I vowed that we would carve out time for them but since I have become more and more politically active, time has become a real problem.

'I make it a condition that I will only accept week-end meetings and public appearances where there are facilities for one or more of the kids to come with me. If I did not they would just get squeezed out. This way they have a sense of what I do when I am not with them and there is no feeling of Daddy disappearing.

'I've noticed more and more MPs bringing their kids to the House. Maybe we are all becoming more conscious of the need to involve our children in our lives.'

D The writer

'My first marriage broke up when Kate and Bonnie were quite young, so I was forced to examine the whole area of fatherhood more closely than I might otherwise have done. I made enormous efforts to stay in touch with the children. My ex-wife and I even experimented with living next door to each other for a while, so they could come and go as they wished, but I think Kate and Bonnie would say now that they found that quite confusing.

'Kate has said in interviews that I was always there for her, but I am not sure I was a very good father. It is true I was around a lot, but, like a lot of Seventies parents, I think I treated the kids as adults too soon. Kate was complaining only the other day that we were too liberal. I think I could have introduced more systems, more order. Instead I took this very loose approach. I regret that now.

'I still worry about my elder daughters as much as I do about my youngest. In that way your kids never leave you.'

E The TV presenter

'I was ready for kids. I'd hit 30, met my wife, we had a lovely house, so we thought, 'Why carry on going to the shops every Saturday spending our money on new sofas, when we could have a kid instead?'

'Having my daughter Betty has forced me to come to terms with who I am and what I am. You feel you are doing something very special when you conceive a child, and you are. But you are also becoming just one more parent in a great long line of parents. It's a great leveller.

'I do resent it occasionally but if ever there is a moment of irritation, it is dispelled by just one look at her. A baby's smile is the greatest self-preservation mechanism in the world. It can melt a grown man.'

*For questions **18–24**, you must choose which of the paragraphs **A–H** on page **76**
fit into the numbered gaps in the following magazine article. There is one extra
paragraph, which does not fit in any of the gaps.*

THE DAY I GAVE UP SMOKING

I thought everyone would be pleased, but one of my colleagues was absolutely furious. 'What do you mean?', she raged. 'If it was that easy, why didn't you stop years ago?'

18

The stop-smoking session was an interesting mixture of group therapy and hypnotherapy and it took place exactly two months and three weeks ago.

19

On that unexceptional Thursday afternoon, I had simply gone along to the Birmingham session of *The Easy Way to Stop Smoking* to write an article about other people trying to give up. 'I shan't be trying to stop myself, it wouldn't be fair,' I announced firmly. 'Since my motivation for being here is writing, not stopping, it would not be right to expect your method to work on me.'

20

We were encouraged to smoke as much as we wished and most of the afternoon was conducted in a room so smoke-filled that we had to open the windows.

21

I suppose what happened was that the stop-smoking messages made intellectual sense. Just as smoking itself had become a challenge in the face of opposition, so the notion of stopping began to feel attractive.

22

In many senses, it was easy. The physical craving, the pangs of desire for nicotine, in just the same place where you feel hunger, faded after a minute or two and I experienced them over only four or five days.

23

Surprisingly, pottering around at home on weekend mornings proved to be the most difficult thing – and it still is.

24

Yes, I *do* miss my cigarettes, but not too much. Each 'new' experience as a non-smoker has to be addressed – eating out, waiting for an aeroplane, booking into a hotel, a theatre interval. All are key moments in which I would have previously smoked cigarettes.

A The possibility of not being a smoker was beginning to make me feel powerful. It was a secret feeling that had nothing to do with anyone except myself. Could I also conquer the world?

B I suppose my inability to explain how one afternoon I had been a packet-a-day, life-long smoker, and four hours later I was not, was faintly irritating. I find it curious myself.

C I am increasingly coming to the view that for me smoking had a great deal to do with displacing boredom; having a cigarette was an activity in itself.

D I could not have been more reasonable. After all, I positively enjoyed smoking. It gave me real pleasure. I thought the counsellor looked at me rather knowingly.

E I had not intended to stop and I did not even particularly want to. For one thing, I wholly resented the remorseless pressure from the anti-smoking mob – and I still do. For another, I had low blood pressure and a long-living and healthy family. I did not cough or feel unwell and threw off colds more easily, it seemed to me, than friends with consciously healthier lifestyles.

F My skin is pinker, I can sing higher notes and I don't smell like a bonfire. People have stopped asking me if I have a sore throat.

G The one activity – my work – that I thought would be the most difficult to accomplish without cigarettes did not cause a single problem. I had really believed that I would not be able to work to deadlines unassisted by nicotine and that for the first time ever I would fail to write a story to order.

H I noticed with interest that when I was told to smoke I was reluctant to do so – and so were the others.

Read the following article from a magazine and answer questions **25–29** *on page* **78**. *Indicate the letter* **A**, **B**, **C** *or* **D** *against the number of each question,* **25–29**. *Give only one answer to each question.*

Tapping into a food supply

In the forests of Madagascar there lives a primate with a lifestyle remarkably like a woodpecker's. Both the woodpecker and the primate, the rare and elusive aye-aye, bore through wood and probe cavities beneath the surface in their search for insect larvae. The woodpecker, of course, uses its beak for chiselling into the wood and its long tongue to extract its prey; the aye-aye, on the other hand, uses its incisor teeth to gnaw its way in and its narrow, elongated third finger to probe and scoop. Though the aye-aye's strange way of feeding was first described over a hundred years ago, scientists have only now discovered how it locates the insects hidden inside the wood.

Dr Carl Erickson, of Duke University's Primate Center, has been investigating the hunting skills of two captive males, Nosferatu and Poe, a female, Samantha, and her infant daughter, Annabelle (*Animal Behaviour*, vol. 41 pp. 793–802). He first tested whether they found insects just by looking for the telltale visual signs of their presence. For example, holes on the surface might indicate sites where female insects had entered the wood and laid their eggs. Dr Erickson presented the aye-ayes with logs in which he had drilled several narrow holes. Some holes led to cavities containing mealworms while others were blank dead-ends. The aye-ayes went straight for the cavities with food, gnawing through the wood and clearly not requiring the visual clues of surface holes.

Perhaps the aye-ayes were locating the mealworms by their smell or the sounds they were making. But further tests showed that they didn't use these clues either. Logs in which the smell of the insects was prevented from leaking out presented no problem, and the aye-ayes also located dead (and therefore silent) mealworms.

If they weren't seeing, smelling or hearing the insects, how were the aye-ayes able to find them? Dr Erickson discovered that they would gnaw down to empty cavities as well as those containing mealworms. They could apparently sense the cavity itself.

When searching for food, an aye-aye taps the surface of the wood with its middle finger and brings its exceptionally large ears forward, focusing them at a point in front of its nose. Dr Erickson suggests that the animal is echo-locating, listening and perhaps feeling for reverberations of the taps that indicate a hollow space below. It can probably also hear the rustle of insects, which might move when disturbed by the tapping from above.

The theory that the aye-aye takes the place of woodpeckers in the woodpecker-free forests of Madagascar is an attractive one. But there are birds, such as the Sickle-billed and Nuthatch Vangas, which do probe for or glean insects from wood, and so the woodpecker niche may not be vacant. Not only can the aye-aye be regarded as a woodpecker and an echo-locating bat rolled into one, but it also behaves like a squirrel (indeed, it was originally classified as one). Its incisors grow continuously like a squirrel's, and it has recently been observed in the wild gnawing through the shells of nuts, and extracting the meat of the nut with its elongated finger.

25 What do the woodpecker and the aye-aye have in common?
- **A** They have exceptionally long tongues.
- **B** They live in the same habitat.
- **C** They have similar eating habits.
- **D** They have strong beaks.

26 The aye-ayes studied by Dr Erickson
- **A** were observed in their natural habitat.
- **B** belonged to one family group.
- **C** had been captured by hunters in Madagascar.
- **D** lived in artificial conditions.

27 Dr Erickson's first hypothesis was that the aye-ayes
- **A** were attracted to female insects and the eggs they laid.
- **B** relied solely on visual senses to locate prey.
- **C** were equally keen to investigate all cavities in wood.
- **D** used their incisors to get faster access to food.

28 What was Dr Erickson's next hypothesis designed to test?
- **A** the degree of development of the aye-aye's sense of touch
- **B** the acuteness of the aye-aye's vision
- **C** the keenness of the aye-aye's sense of hearing
- **D** the role of smell in the aye-aye's search for food

29 Why was the aye-aye once considered to be a squirrel?
- **A** It hoards nuts for the winter.
- **B** It lives in trees.
- **C** It has an unusual way of feeding.
- **D** Its teeth don't stop growing.

25 ....

26 ....

27 ....

28 ....

29 ....

FOURTH TEXT/QUESTIONS 30–41

Answer questions **30–41** by choosing from the reviews **A–I** printed on this page and on page **80**.
Note: When more than one answer is required, these may be given **in any order**. Some choices may be required more than once.

Which play is described as being

a change from the author's previous work? **30** ....

performed too infrequently? **31** ....

shorter than the original? **32** ....

almost a disaster? **33** ....

sometimes lacking in pace? **34** ....

Which production or productions provide an opportunity to see or hear

an action-packed performance? **35** ....

a highly-recommended comedy? **36** .... **37** ....

a newly-written work? **38** .... **39** ....

a mixture of sadness and comedy? **40** ....

a play about the role of women in society? **41** ....

THEATRE
CHARLES SPENCER

A Tamburlaine the Great
Marlowe's ten-act epic about the all-conquering warrior can seem never-ending, but it emerges as one of the most thrilling nights of the year in Terry Hands' staging. He has hacked great chunks from the text and offers a production that combines the glories of Marlowe's play with an exhilarating speed and physicality. Antony Sher is in terrific form in the title role, somersaulting from the balcony, sliding down a rope head-first as he delivers a speech, demanding and getting the audience's complete attention as his eyes glint with a mad lust for power and glory. Great stuff.
Swan Theatre, Stratford-upon-Avon (01789 295623)

B Women Laughing
Welcome London transfer for the late Michael Wall's fine play, seen at the Manchester Royal Exchange in May. The first act creates an atmosphere of unsettling menace as two married couples chat on a sunny suburban lawn. In the second half, the location shifts and the piece becomes a powerful, compassionate study of the devastating effects of illness. The British theatre lost a talent of great promise when Wall died at the tragically early age of 44.
Royal Court Theatre, London SW1 (0171 730 1745)

C Amphibians
Billy Roche is the latest in

the long line of Irish dramatists to have enriched the English stage. All his plays to date have been set in his native Wexford, and this latest piece explores the decline of the fishing industry with his usual mixture of rich characterisation, painful emotion and sudden moments of quirky humour. The play sprawls a bit aimlessly at times, but builds to a blistering climax.

Barbican's Pit Theatre, London EC2 (0171 638 8891)

D Murder by Misadventure
Traditional thriller involving our old friend, 'the perfect murder'. This time it is Gerald Harper and William Gaunt who play the crime-writing partnership intent on killing each other, and though it's all rather familiar stuff, the twists and turns are handled with ingenuity.

Whitehall Theatre, London SW1 (0171 867 1119)

E The Alchemist
Young director Sam Mendes finds the gold in Jonson's great comedy of 17th-century confidence tricksters. First seen at the *Swan* in Stratford last year,

the show works just as well on the Barbican's main stage, with Jonathan Hyde, David Bradley and Joanne Pearce repeating their fine performances as the wicked trio of con-artists.

Barbican Theatre, London EC2 (0171 638 8891)

F The Madras House
Peter James' production of Harley Granville Barker's rich, panoramic comedy about fashion and the position of women in Edwardian society transfers to London after its success at the Edinburgh Festival. The staging is stylish, the acting excellent, the play itself an unjustly neglected classic.

Lyric Theatre, Hammersmith, London W6 (0181 741 2311)

G Dreams from a summer house
This delightful new musical finds playwright Alan Ayckbourn in unusually benign form as he relocates the *Beauty and the Beast* story deep in the heart of London suburbia. A lush score by John Pattison and an unashamedly schmaltzy celebration of romantic love combine to make this good-hearted show a real

winner. London impresarios looking for a hit should board the next train to Scarborough.

Stephen Joseph Theatre, Scarborough (01723 370541)

H The Merry Wives of Windsor
David Thacker's lacklustre production of Shakespeare's most farcical comedy came perilously close to being awarded the dreaded thumbs-down symbol, but this disappointing, crudely designed show is redeemed by first-rate comic performances from Ron Cook as the French physician Dr Caius and Anton Lesser as the explosively jealous husband, Ford. Almost everyone else looks faintly embarrassed, as well they might.

Shakespeare Theatre, Stratford-upon-Avon (01789 295623)

I The Voysey Inheritance
Another major Granville Barker revival, now touring the regions. This story of an apparently respectable solicitor who bequeaths a corrupt financial legacy to his son results in a marvellous play.

Apollo Theatre, Oxford (01865 244544)

PAPER 2 WRITING (2 hours)

*This paper contains one Section A task and four Section B tasks. You must complete the Section A task and **one** from Section B, using an appropriate style for each task.*
The two sections carry equal marks.
*Read the task instructions and consider the information **carefully** both for Section A and the task which you select for Section B.*

SECTION A

1 *You spent your last vacation acting as a team leader at a summer camp for young people in Canada. Other members of your English club are thinking of doing the same thing this year, and the secretary of the club has asked you to write a report based on your experiences and those of other team leaders so that new team leaders know what to expect.*

*Read the advertisement with your comments below and, on page **82**, the notes which you made after talking to other team leaders. Then, **using the information carefully**, write the **report**.*

*Your report should be about **250** words long.*

Canada Camp

Want to visit Canada but short of money?
Canada Camp is the way to do it.
We're looking for suitable people to work as team leaders
in camps throughout Canada.

We need people who:

including the camp leader – not easy! / get on with other people
are enthusiastic — *and patience!*
have plenty of energy
swimming, climbing or riding essential / have skills they can pass on to others
love the countryside —— *wonderful scenery*
are looking for **adventure**

We offer:

no transport from airport to camp / return air ticket — *dormitory with the kids*
meals and accommodation
pocket money — *gained 3 kgs!*
the experience of a lifetime!

81

CANADA CAMP NOTES

1. Large group of kids, 8–12 years old – very different interests; not much time for self, sometimes felt more like school teacher – but a couple of the kids still keep in touch (J.B.)

2. 'Pocket money' was just that – not much use for seeing Canada afterwards; had to borrow from father (M.-J.C.)

3. Weather more changeable than expected – had to buy a raincoat! A few very hot days (P.D.)

4. Nearly had accident on the river – no-one trained to handle a canoe … luckily Maria has life-saving certificate! An awful lot of responsibility really (T.L.S.)

5. Primitive conditions but a lot of fun – pity there was nowhere to buy film for my camera! (S.G.)

SECTION B

*Choose **one** of the following writing tasks. Your answers should follow exactly the instructions given.*
*Write approximately **250** words.*

2 An increasing number of tourists are coming to visit your town. Your local tourist office is producing a series of leaflets to help tourists make the most of their visit. You have been asked to write a leaflet for visitors who have only a morning or afternoon to spend in your town.

   Write the **leaflet**, recommending what they should do and why.

3 You recently attended a music festival or concert and want to write about it to an English-speaking friend who has the same or similar tastes as you. Write him/her a **letter** about the event and explain how it did or did not come up to your expectations.

4 A US company has asked you to write a brief practical **guide** to behaviour in business situations in your country. You should refer to appropriate ways of dressing, how to address people and how business people meet socially. Add any other comments on aspects of business behaviour in your country which you think would be useful.

   Write the **guide**.

5 You have seen the following on your college notice-board:

> *THEFT is on the increase.*
> *Have you got any ideas that will help students protect their personal property?*
> *Your college magazine needs an article on this topic and is offering the latest Sherlock Holmes video for the best article.*

   Write the **article**, in which you put forward some suggestions on what students can do to protect their possessions.

PAPER 3 ENGLISH IN USE (1 hour 30 minutes)

This paper requires you to complete six tasks.
Answer all questions.
The total number of questions for tasks 1 to 5 is 63; the last task is numbered 81–89.

SECTION A

1 *For questions 1–15, read the text below and then decide which word on page 85 best fits each space. Circle the letter you choose for each question. The exercise begins with an example (0).*

CRIME – REVERSING THE TREND

Crime, as we are all (**0**) ... , has been a growing problem all over the world in the last thirty years. But we are not (**1**) ... against crime. Much is being done – and more can be done – to reverse the trend. You can play a part in it.

The first step towards preventing crime is understanding its (**2**) ... . Most crime is against property, not (**3**) ... , and most crime is not carried out by professionals; nor is it carefully planned. Property crimes (**4**) ... on the easy opportunity. They are often (**5**) ... by adolescents and young men, the majority of whom stop offending as they grow older – the (**6**) ... age for offending is fifteen. Also, and not surprisingly, the (**7**) ... of being a victim of crime (**8**) ... greatly depending on where you live.

This (**9**) ... by criminals on the easy opportunity is the (**10**) ... to much crime prevention. Motor cars, for example, are a sitting target for the criminal. Surveys have shown that approximately one in five drivers do not always (**11**) ... to secure their cars by locking all the doors and shutting all the windows, and in 30 per cent of domestic burglaries the burglar simply walks in without having to use (**12**) ... . If opportunities like these did not exist, criminals would have a much harder time. The chances are that many crimes would not be committed, which would release more police time for (**13**) ... serious crime.

Of course, the primary responsibility for (**14**) ... with crime rests with the police and the courts, but, if you care about improving the (**15**) ... of life for yourself and your community, there are many ways you can help reverse the trend.

---

0 Ⓐ aware   **B** conscious   **C** informed   **D** known

	A	B	C	D
1	unprepared	hopeless	powerless	weak
2	nature	type	reason	method
3	the victim	the public	residents	citizens
4	increase	thrive	develop	happen
5	performed	started	committed	done
6	peak	major	maximum	top
7	percentage	seriousness	rate	risk
8	varies	adapts	transformed	adjusts
9	awareness	seizing	reliance	taking
10	answer	method	way	key
11	trouble	bother	care	ensure
12	force	threat	tools	tricks
13	removing	facing	tackling	dealing
14	containing	destroying	fighting	coping
15	quality	peacefulness	enjoyment	way

In the examination, your answer on the answer sheet would look like this:

0	A	0
		▢ ▢

2 *For questions* **16–30***, complete the following article by writing each missing word in the space provided.* **Use only one word for each space***. The exercise begins with an example* (**0**).

HERBS AND SPICES

There is nothing new in the use of herbs and spices. They have enriched human life for thousands of years, (**0**) ..p̲r̲o̲v̲i̲d̲i̲n̲g̲.. both comfort and luxury. They have flavoured our food, cured our ailments and surrounded us (**16**) .... sweet scents. They have also played (**17**) .... part in our folklore and magic. It (**18**) .... be a very different world without them.

Nobody really knows who first used herbs and spices, or for (**19**) .... purpose. All their properties were known to the ancient Greeks and Egyptians and to (**20**) .... living in early Biblical times. The knowledge that they employed, and that we (**21**) ....use today, must have been based on the trial and error (**22**) .... early man, who was originally drawn to the plants (**23**) .... of their tantalising aroma. He gradually discovered their individual effects (**24**) .... his food and well-being and our use of them comes from those early experiments. For centuries herbs and spices were appreciated to the full but in modern times the arrival of (**25**) .... convenience foods and new medicines of the twentieth century almost (**26**) .... us forget them. But anything (**27**) .... has been so much loved and valued (**28**) .... never be completely neglected. The knowledge has been kept alive and (**29**) .... our present-day search (**30**) .... all things natural, herbs and spices have come into their own again.

In the examination, your answer on the answer sheet would look like this:

0	providing	0
		▭ ▭

SECTION B

3   *In **most** lines of the following text, there is **either** a spelling **or** a punctuation error. For each numbered line **31–47**, write the correctly spelled word(s) or show the correct punctuation next to the question number below. **Some** lines are correct. Indicate these lines with a tick (√). The exercise begins with two examples (**0**).*

0	When Deansgate was a narrow street and the sight of
0	Central Station was a squalid slum, Wood Street Mission was
31	founded. In 1869, according to a contempry police
32	officer, the neighbourhood was 'the rendezvous of thieves,
33	the worst haunt of vice'. In the Mission building hundred's
34	of meals were served and thousands of pears of shoes
35	given away. At Christmas four hundred tramps, and
36	criminals came to a meal and a service; in the
37	summer hundreds of children queud to be taken out
38	for a day at the seaside. Every night the streets
39	were searched for homeless boys sleeping in door ways
40	and under market stalls. They were given beds in
41	Wood Street Jobs were found for them and many were
42	sent to live in canada. The new Superintendent
43	in 1892 was an excriminal and he founded a
44	holiday camp at St Anne's-on-Sea wich could
45	accommodate a hundred an twenty children. Many
46	local residence still remember happy holidays there. The
47	Mission still provides about a thousand familys a year
	with clothing and helps or advises many more.

Examples: **0**   ..*site*......
          0   .√..........   **36** ....   **42** ....
          31 ....   **37** ....   **43** ....
          32 ....   **38** ....   **44** ....
          33 ....   **39** ....   **45** ....
          34 ....   **40** ....   **46** ....
          35 ....   **41** ....   **47** ....

In the examination, your answer on the answer sheet would look like this:

0	site	0 ▭ ▭
0	✓	0 ▭ ▭

4 For questions **48–56**, read the following teacher's comments on a school project. Use the information in it to complete the numbered gaps in the informal letter from the student who did the project. **Use not more than one word for each gap**. Then write the new words in the space provided. The words which you need **do not occur** in the teacher's comments. The exercise begins with an example (**0**).

TEACHER'S COMMENTS

CONTENT:	Margaret's report on 'Language Development in Two-Year-Old Twins' represents a year's painstaking work. The case-study shows acute observation but the material could have been more efficiently organised. The paper was perhaps over-ambitious since it extended to 10,000 words instead of the recommended 5,000.
STYLE:	The writing is lively but sometimes too colloquial for this kind of text. Margaret needs to be more aware of refinements of meaning; occasionally she is inaccurate in her choice of vocabulary, with unfortunate results.
PRESENTATION:	The project is pleasantly illustrated with photographs and some useful charts though it is a pity these were not original material. The work is marred by a number of typing and/or spelling errors and would have benefited from stricter proof-reading before submission.

INFORMAL LETTER

Dear Annie,

How are you getting on with your language project? I have just seen the notes on mine from my English teacher but I can't (0) ..say.. yet whether I've passed or not. She seems (48) .... with the research but she says it is rather (49) .... and much too (50) .... She thinks I use too much (51) .... and sometimes quite the (52) .... words! Because the horrid woman (53) .... the pictures she thinks I (54) .... them from books. I expect she's right, though, when she says there are (55) .... of spelling mistakes; I should have let Mum read it before I (56) .... it in! I hope yours goes down better — let me know what the teacher says,

Love,
Marge

In the examination, your answer on the answer sheet would look like this:

0	say	0
		⎯ ⎯

SECTION C

5   For questions **57–63** *read through the following text and then choose the best phrase given below it to fill leach of the blanks. Write one letter (**A–K**) in the space provided.* **Some of the suggested answers do not fit at all.** *The exercise begins with an example (**0**).*

FINDING FISH

Fish are like any other living creature, in that they react in a number of different ways to the weather. The heat of the water in which they live (**0**) ... are the two most important factors we have to consider when we try to find fish.

Fish can rise or sink into the deep water according to the temperature (**57**) ... . They can also seek life-giving oxygen by moving closer to places (**58**) ... , such as waterfalls, fast-running streams and streams that run into a lake. Rainfall and wind sweeping across a lake also bring oxygen into the water, (**59**) ... . Some fish do not need the same quantities of oxygen as others, so they are found in deep lakes (**60**) ... . The trees drop an enormous number of leaves into the lake every winter. These decay, releasing dangerous gas.

In winter, we find that the warmest water is at the bottom of lakes and ponds. Fish tend to feed right at the bottom. Some stop feeding altogether as the cold months arrive, falling into a state of partial hibernation, (**61**) ... . In summertime, we find a complete reversal of water temperature. The warmest water is just under the surface of the lake. As the depth becomes greater, so the water gets a lot colder. Fish that use little oxygen can rise to feed near the top of the water, (**62**) ... .

Rivers are much less affected by hot weather. They are fed by water that seeps through the ground, (**63**) ... and therefore not absorbing heat as still water does.

A	often surrounded by trees	**G**	coming out only on occasional sunny days
B	constantly on the move		
C	and the amount of oxygen available to them	**H**	that cause oxygen to be taken into the water
D	and generally they are swept across the lake to the windy side	**I**	for warm water contains less oxygen than colder water
E	that they find most comfortable	**J**	to the deeper parts of the lake
F	to be replaced by warmer water	**K**	making the living conditions better for the inhabitants

In the examination, your answer on the answer sheet would look like this:

0	*C*		0
			▭ ▭

6 *You have been asked to prepare a short article about football for an encyclopaedia. Read the notes below and write **one sentence only** for each numbered set of notes, using connecting words and phrases as appropriate. You may add words and change the form of the words given in the notes, but do not add any extra information. The first point has been expanded for you as an example (**0**).*

Football

0 Popular, played and watched throughout world: Africa – Latin America; USA – Arab States

81 Team game (11-a-side), ball, grass pitch

82 Pitch = 90-120 m x 45-90 m; goal each end 7.3 m x 2.4 m

83 Object – move ball (feet or head) to score goal

84 No hands on ball (except goalkeeper)

85 Similar game – ancient times (Greeks, Chinese, Egyptians, Romans): modern game not until early 19th C.

86 Cambridge Univ. – standard rules, 1848; Football Association est. 1863

87 1st World Cup – Uruguay, 1930; now every 4 yrs, USA 1994

88 Different kinds – rugby, American, 'Australian Rules' (18 players per side), Gaelic (15 players per side)

89 Now most important spectator sport (world) – 'superstars', paid $$$$

Example: 0 Football is a popular game which is played and watched throughout the world from Africa to Latin America, from the USA to the Arab States.

81

82

83

84

85

86

87

88

89

PAPER 4 LISTENING (approximately 45 minutes)

This paper requires you to listen to a selection of recorded material and answer the accompanying questions.
*There are four sections to the test, **A**, **B**, **C** and **D**. You will hear Section B **once** only. All the other parts of the test will be heard twice. During the test there will be a pause before each section to allow you to look through the questions, and other pauses to let you think about your answers.*

SECTION A

You will hear part of a radio programme on food. Janet, a journalist who specialises in cookery, is giving a talk about bread.
*As you listen, complete the notes on Janet's talk for questions **1–10**.*
You will hear the recording twice.

AMOUNT OF BREAD EATEN

Last year consumption ☐ **1** ☐ by ☐ **2** ☐

In previous ten years consumption ☐ **3** ☐

by ☐ **4** ☐ per cent

OTHER CHANGES

Bread was made with bleached flour.

Is now often made with ☐ **5** ☐ flour.

Change because people believe this is ☐ **6** ☐

Influences on tastes are ☐ **7** ☐ and ☐ **8** ☐

Ingredients in bread making

	rye flour
9	
10	
	softened grains

SECTION B

You will hear an introduction to a course in Business Management Today.
As you listen, fill in the information for questions **11–21**, *using a number or a few words.*
Listen very carefully as you will hear this piece only **once**.

BUSINESS MANAGEMENT TODAY

Seminar/Workshop Programme

MARKETING	**11**
12	Bishop's Hall One
STRATEGIC PLANNING	Bishop's Hall Two
HUMAN RESOURCES	**13**

TIMETABLE	*LOCATION*
9.30 – 11.00	Convocation Hall
Coffee and biscuits	**14**
11.30 – 1.00	**15**
Lunch	**16**
2.00 – 3.30	**17**
Tea and biscuits	
4.00 – 5.30	**18**
5.30 – 6.30	**19**

NB Books and resource materials

on display in **20**

Centre closes **21**

SECTION C

You will hear two employers, Tim Lloyd and Sally Taylor, being interviewed about the subject of commercial sponsorship for students. During the discussion various comments are made.
For questions 22–28, indicate which comments are made by Tim and which are made by Sally. You may write both initials, or one initial, or neither as an answer. Write T (for Tim), S (for Sally) or N (for Neither).
You will hear the discussion twice.

22 Businesses will increasingly seek to appoint more graduates to managerial positions.

22 [   ]

23 Sponsored students receive approximately £700 a year in financial help.

23 [   ]

24 It doesn't matter which subject a student has chosen to study.

24 [   ]

25 A lot of students accept the cash but have no intention of joining the company later.

25 [   ]

26 A sponsored student is under no obligation to join the company after graduation.

26 [   ]

27 It is likely that business will gradually replace government sponsorship of students.

27 [   ]

28 Students seeking sponsorship should make it clear how the company will benefit from the relationship.

28 [   ]

You will hear various people talking about the weather.

TASK ONE

For questions 29–33, match the extracts with the people listed A–H.

A a pilot

B a postman

C an architect

D a camper

E a farmer

F a gardener

G a nurse

H a builder

29	
30	
31	
32	
33	

TASK TWO

For questions 34–38, match the extract with the weather conditions A–H.

A fog

B ice

C drought

D hail

E wind

F cloud

G rain

H snow

34	
35	
36	
37	
38	

You will hear the recording twice.

PAPER 5 SPEAKING (23 minutes)

There will be two examiners, one acting as an Interlocutor and one as an Assessor. You will be examined together with two other candidates. One of you will be Candidate A, the second will be Candidate B and the third will be Candidate C.

Phase A (approximately 5 minutes)

You and your two partners will talk about yourselves and each other. You will be asked to find out and offer information about you or your partners' background, interests, career plans, etc.

Phase B (approximately 5–6 minutes)

You will each be given the opportunity to talk for a minute.
You will each be given a picture to talk about (Lifestyles and people) and you will be asked to talk about it in a particular way. The Interlocutor will explain this in full. You will be asked to show your picture to your partners while you are talking about it and your partners will be asked to listen carefully to what is being said. The pictures are to be found in the centre section of this book on p. C16.
Candidate A will be given a picture first and will have one minute to talk about it.
Then Candidate B will be given a different picture and will have one minute to talk about it.
Then Candidate C will be given a different picture again and will have one minute to talk about it.
You will then be asked to look at each other's pictures again and say whether or not you agree with what you have each said. You will have about two minutes to talk together.

Phase C (5–6 minutes)

The Interlocutor will place a new set of pictures (Environment competition) on pp. C14 and C15 between you and your partners. These pictures provide the basis for a discussion between you and your partners.
The Interlocutor will give instructions and you will have five or six minutes for this.

Phase D (5–6 minutes)

This will be based on what you have discussed in Phase C. You will be invited to report the outcome of your discussion saying whether you agree or not with your partners. You will then take part in a more general discussion based on what has been discussed in Phase C. Both the Interlocutor and the Assessor will take part in this discussion.
Please note: this test may be conducted with two partners only. In this case only two pictures should be used and the time allowed for each phase of the test will be the same as those given for Practice Test 1, Paper 5 on page 25.

Answer sheet for Paper 1 Reading

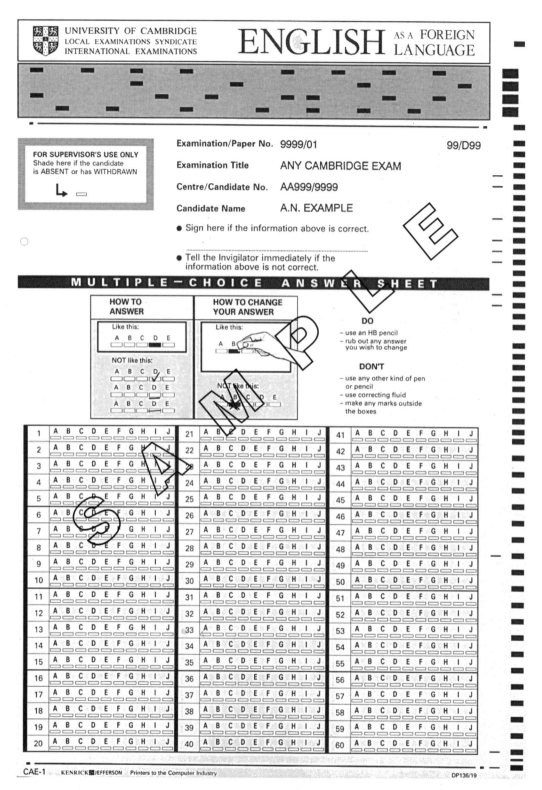

You may photocopy this page.

© UCLES/K&J

Answer sheet for Paper 3 English in Use

[This is the first sheet only]

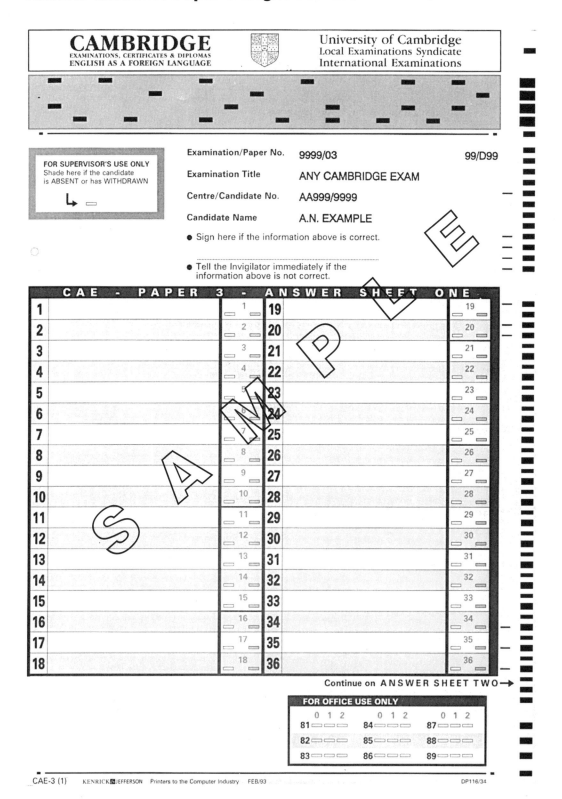

You may photocopy this page.

© UCLES/K&J

Answer sheet for Paper 3 English in Use (second sheet)

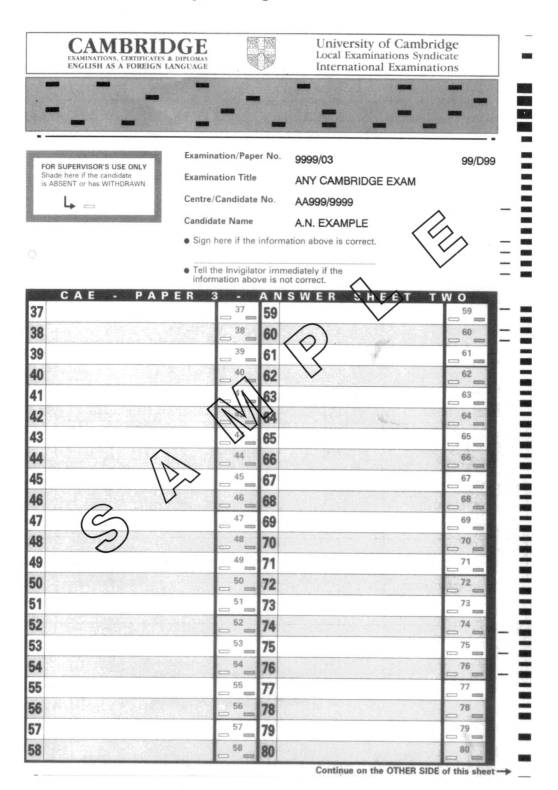

You may photocopy this page.

© UCLES/K&J

FOR
OFFICE
USE
ONLY

81 _____

82 _____

83 _____

84 _____

85 _____

86 _____

87 _____

88 _____

89 _____

You may photocopy this page.

© UCLES/K&J

Answer sheet for Paper 4 Listening

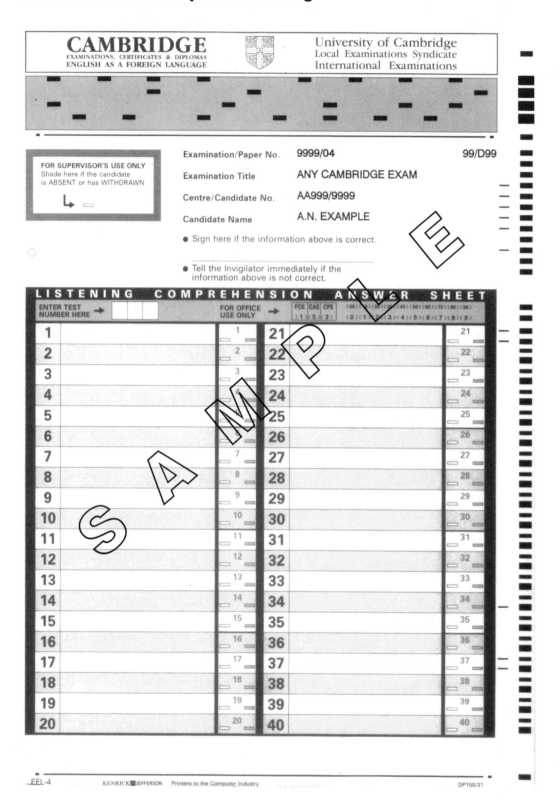

You may photocopy this page.

© UCLES/K&J

100